_Ki..._

"The truism that families con... illuminated with haunting beauty ... in this ... comedy-drama ... a piercing p...rait of the contempora... social architecture, in which the dis...... between people can be widened or collapsed with disorienting ease, whether it is through the click of a keyboard, a telephone conversation or a chance encounter. Many of the characters in the play never actually meet, and yet we come away with a moving sense of how each individual's experience resonates – troublingly or happily – in the lives of almost everyone else." – *NY Times*

"... compelling ... [an] expanding web of relationships is examined primarily for the better, illuminated with humor and insight in a series of concise, effective, emotion-laden vignettes ... Doran's dialogue is pointed and humorous...KIN is both entertaining and thoughtful, a satisfying emotional journey from start to finish." – *Associated Press*

Parents' Evening

"Doran's script shows insightful nuance!" – *NYTheatre.com*

"The strength of Parents' Evening is in the dialogue, specifically the insights that Doran reveals about the highs and lows, connections and alienations, of a couple with a child." – *Theatre is Easy*

Mystery of Love & Sex

"Perfectly wonderful! Among the season's finest plays. It is tender, funny, packed with humanity and brimming with surprising revelations. Bathsheba Doran has written a play with such compassion and wry wisdom that I emerged from the theater into yet another frigid day feeling warmed from within." – *The New York Times*

"Wise and exquisitely crafted." – *Time Out New York*

"The best new play of this young year." – *Deadline.com*

Bathsheba Doran

THE MARRIAGE PLAYS

Kin
Parents' Evening
The Mystery of Love and Sex

OBERON BOOKS
LONDON

WWW.OBERONBOOKS.COM

This collection first published in 2016 by Oberon Books Ltd
521 Caledonian Road, London N7 9RH
Tel: +44 (0) 20 7607 3637 / Fax: +44 (0) 20 7607 3629
e-mail: info@oberonbooks.com
www.oberonbooks.com

Collection copyright © Bathsheba Doran, 2016

Kin © Bathsheba Doran, 2012, *Parents' Evening* © Bathsheba
Doran, 2015, *The Mystery of Love and Sex* © Bathsheba Doran, 2016.

Bathsheba Doran is hereby identified as author of these plays
in accordance with section 77 of the Copyright, Designs and
Patents Act 1988. The author has asserted her moral rights.

All rights whatsoever in this play are strictly reserved and
application for performance etc. should be made before
commencement of rehearsal to Mark Subias, United Talent
Agency, 888 Seventh Avenue, 9th Floor, New York, NY 10106,
USA (Subias_M@unitedtalent.com). No performance may be
given unless a licence has been obtained, and no alterations may
be made in the title or the text of the play without the author's
prior written consent.

You may not copy, store, distribute, transmit, reproduce or
otherwise make available this publication (or any part of it) in
any form, or binding or by any means (print, electronic, digital,
optical, mechanical, photocopying, recording or otherwise),
without the prior written permission of the publisher. Any person
who does any unauthorized act in relation to this publication may
be liable to criminal prosecution and civil claims for damages.

A catalogue record for this book is available from the British
Library.

PB ISBN: 9781783197590
E ISBN: 9781783197606

Cover image © Juulijs

Visit www.oberonbooks.com to read more about all our books
and to buy them. You will also find features, author interviews and
news of any author events, and you can sign up for e-newsletters
so that you're always first to hear about our new releases.

For my parents

Contents

Introduction

I never wanted to write about marriage. It annoyed me greatly when someone pointed out that it was a recurring theme in my plays. How very *female*, I thought. How *dated*. "Marriage in Nineteenth Century Women's Literature", a lecture I would have skipped in college.

Well, I can't help it. I'm obsessed with marriage. For me, there is nothing domestic or trivial about it. It is the terror of loneliness, the instinct to love, the horror of intimacy, the primitive desire to band together, the nightmare of a trap, the glimpse of utopia, the compromises life forces on us, our need for allies in a wilderness. Marriage is a great plain of emotion that takes place in private, little rooms.

Like most people, the first marriage I knew intimately was my parents'. In it I witnessed such deep love, such despair, such kindnesses and such anger, such loyalties and absurdities, such negotiations and selfishness, such strength and fragility that it formed my sense of marriage as high drama.

The next marriage I knew intimately was my own, or rather the beginning of my own. I found my late father-in-law's copy of *Kin* recently. I had written in the flyleaf "this is a play about how much I love your daughter and how long it took me to find her." I finished *Kin* a month before my own wedding. Like Sean and Anna in the play, I chose a partner from an entirely different background. I watched the extraordinary process of our individual families merging, all the time wondering how and why the offspring of two such different universes had managed to come together and build their own new world. I had no idea if my marriage would last and *Kin* is no love story convinced of it's own happy ending. It was a hard play to write: an experiment in structure and, though the oldest story there is – boy meets girl – I tried to tell it the way it feels when you are actually going through it. Falling in love, a friend said to me, is like having someone poking around the dark corners of your house where you don't want anyone to look. It's terrifying.

The Mystery of Love and Sex was even harder to write but hard in a different way. Although the play is a marriage play the lead character, Charlotte, is not heterosexual. Until this play I had resisted writing what might be considered a "gay play." I was concerned that creatively it would prevent me accessing the universal. I was concerned professionally it would leave me pigeon-holed and marginalized. But once again, my subconscious would have none of it. A few months after my wife and I had our first son, this play forced its way out of me. To a certain extent it brings together all the themes and obsessions of the other two plays in this volume. Like *Parents' Evening, The Mystery of Love and Sex* is about one of the frequent by-products of a marriage: navigating your children. This time I was able to write from the vantage point of a parent, not a child. Like *Kin*, the play is about falling in love. More than anything else though, *The Mystery of Love and Sex* is about friendship. Charlotte and Jonny are the lovers of the play and although theirs is not the wedding at the play's end, theirs is the marriage that the audience witness. Because, after all, as the Father says in *Parents' Evening,* isn't that what a marriage is? Best friends?

Bathsheba Doran
New York, 2016

KIN

Kin was presented by Playwrights Horizons (Tim Sanford, Artistic Director; Leslie Marcus, Managing Director; Carol Fishman, General Manager) in New York City, opening on March 21, 2011. It was directed by Sam Gold; with sets by Paul Steinberg; costumes by David Zinn; lights by Jane Cox; sound by Matt Tierney; the dialect coach was Stephen Gabis; the Production Manager was Christopher Boll; and the Production Stage Manager was Alaina Taylor. The cast was as follows:

LINDA	Suzanne Bertish
MAX	Bill Buell
ANNA	Kristen Bush
SEAN	Patch Darragh
KAY	Kit Flanagan
HELENA	Laura Heisler
SIMON/GIDEON	Matthew Rauch
ADAM	Cotter Smith
RACHEL	Molly Ward

Characters

Anna (30s)

Adam, Anna's father (60s)

Helena, (30s)

Sean (30s)

Linda, Sean's mother (55-65)

Max, Linda's brother (55-65)

Rachel (30s)

Kay (60s)

Gideon (34)

Simon (40s)

(GIDEON and SIMON should be played by the same actor. This should not be emphasized, but an unrecognizable transformation is not required.)

Time and Place

The action of the play takes place over the last seven years in various locations in America and Ireland.

A Note on Design

When I began writing I thought of this play as taking place in what I found myself referring to as "the landscape of the mind." Many of my characters were based in what I only thought of as "the city". It could have been any major Western Capital – New York, Paris, London, or an imaginary city entirely. Other characters were simply placed "far away." I was attempting to conjure the globe. Eventually I found it helped the story to be specific so now there is a literal geography, but I hope that the director and design team will help recapture my early sense that this play was taking place above all in a non-literal landscape.

A Note on Staging

This is a play made from largely two person scenes that is none-the-less about an ensemble. To underline this my original idea was to have the entire cast on stage for every scene except the first and last. Sam Gold refined this suggestion into something more delicate, complex and idiosyncratic. I now think it suffices to say that I hope future directors will find their own way to maintain a sense of ensemble so that we feel all characters throughout, hidden sometimes, in shadows maybe, but present.

"What can I say? God help me, what can I say?
Silence will stifle me ..."
Sophocles, *Electra*

"I saw a crow running about with a stork. I marveled long
and investigated their case in order that I might find the clue
as to what is was that they had in common. When amazed
and bewildered I approached them then indeed I saw
that both of them were lame."
Rumi, *Spiritual Couplets*

"A man who calls his kinsman to a feast does not do so to save
them from starving. They all have food in their own homes.
When we gather together in the moonlit village ground it is not
because of the moon. Every man can see it in his own compound.
We come together because it is good for kinsman to do so."
Chinua Achebe, *Things Fall Apart*

SCENE ONE
AN OFFICE AT COLUMBIA UNIVERSITY

ANNA sits. SIMON stands. Everything awkward, uncomfortable.

SIMON: I thought it was best not to leave you dangling, you
know? But at this stage of life ... I mean ... I know what
I'm looking for, you know what you're looking for, we
know what we're looking for, or maybe we don't, maybe
that's the thing, maybe I don't know what I'm looking for
but I know it's not you. That sounds terrible, doesn't it? But
no, fuck it, I'm trying to be truthful here, let's have truth in
human relations for once, how about that? Let's be truthful
with one another. I mean did you think this was going
anywhere? Really?

ANNA shakes her head.

Thank you. Thank you. Now I feel less like an ass. And I
mean – I'm so much older than you, that's probably why
you picked me, right? A father figure? You lost your dad
when you were very young, right? So that was probably
part of the attraction, don't you think? But that's not
healthy, that's not sustainable, or maybe it is, I don't
know.

ANNA: My father's still alive.

SIMON: Oh. Then I'm confusing you with someone else.
Sorry. Of course he is.

The point is – and this is where I'm the real asshole –
I don't know what I want. Not really. I mean, sometimes
I think I want something long term, but I've *been* married,
you know? And it was no fun. Now maybe that was her,
maybe that was me, maybe it was the combination but ...
but ... I just want someone I can talk to, you know?
And fuck. And we *had* that. I'm not denying it. We had
that. But now ... it's over, isn't it? I mean the conversation
is over. Can't you just feel it? There's something dead here.
The light's gone out. And if the light's gone out then put
out the light. Or maybe not. I don't know ... we could try

7

to ignite it. But love shouldn't be so much effort.
Or maybe it should. It's such a fucking construct, you
know? Literature is such a fucking *trap*. Unrealistic
expectations. I don't know. I'm just so fucking lonely.
And I know you are too, maybe that's what brought us
together, right? Loneliness. A love of Keats. Your mind,
you have a fucking brilliant mind, you know that? Your
thesis is fucking brilliant. You're going to have an incredible
career, and you'll forget all about me! I'll just be some old
professor of yours that you inveigled into bed with your
skinny arms and your brilliant mind. Because let's be real.
We admire each other but … this is even a little sordid.
The rest of the faculty knows, I think. Clancy made a veiled
comment … and it's not against the rules, exactly, you
are an adjunct and this *is* the English department, we are
all poets here, and poets fuck, but Clancy's comment … I
think fundamentally … it made me feel cheap. And it made
you … cheap by association … So I think ….You haven't
said anything … Are you going to make this hard on me?
Don't. Please don't. This is just human relationships. I
wrote a poem once. When I was in my thirties and I still
wrote poetry. And I compared a woman's vagina to a
revolving door. People come in. They go out. That's life.
And you know what my simile for the penis was? A staple
gun. In an office. Punch, punch, punch. Revolve, revolve,
revolve. That is life. That is the fucking monotony of
searching for your soul mate. OK? I still stand by that. So
just … Did we even love each other?

ANNA: No.

*SIMON stares at ANNA, hoping for a better cue to exit. He doesn't get
one. So he sighs and leaves.*

SCENE TWO
CENTRAL PARK

Midnight.

HELENA on the grass, cradling a dead dog. Paroxysms of grief.

HELENA: Zoë! Don't be dead, don't be dead, don't be dead.
I love you, I will always love you. Oh my dog! My life
partner! My love! How could you die? How could you
die and leave me here! I don't even know what to do with
your body! They say it's illegal to bury you in the park!
You loved the park! They say, they say if I don't have any
money I should put you in a bag, in a big black bag, and I
should write on the bag "dead dog" and leave you out with
the garbage as if you weren't a *soul*! As if you weren't *my*
soul!

Her cell phone rings.

(Into the phone:) Anna? Where are you? Where the fuck
are you? I need you, Anna, I need you to get here. I'm
freaking out, I'm too upset, I can't even see. Tears are
literally blinding me. Plus it's dark. Totally. You're right.
I'm overreacting. Well, you kind of sound like you think
I'm overreacting.

*And now we see ANNA on her cell phone. HELENA does not see her.
ANNA does not see HELENA. ANNA has a flashlight.*

*She turns and the beam from her flashlight hits the sorry sight of
HELENA and her dead dog.*

HELENA: There you are.

ANNA: Here I am.

HELENA: *(Eternally grateful.)* You brought a flashlight.
So practical.

ANNA: Can I see Zoë? *(She looks at the dog.)* She looks peaceful.

HELENA: You think?

ANNA: Absolutely.

HELENA: I brought a …

HELENA produces an inadequate gardening tool.

ANNA: Do you want me to dig?

HELENA: I'll dig the grave. She was my dog.

ANNA: Of course.

HELENA: Keep watch. Fucking city regulations, I mean what the fuck, it's sick, it's Greek, it's … what happened to universal space? Isn't it my fucking planet? Wasn't it Zoë's fucking earth? I mean, why does everybody seem to own a piece of the universe but me. Well fuck that, my earth, my dirt, my tax dollars.

HELENA digs. Eventually …

ANNA: The last open grave I saw was my mom's.

HELENA: You know what I'm feeling … because your mom … I mean it's probably not the same. Your mom. My dog. That's really offensive.

Beat.

ANNA: I know what you're feeling.

HELENA: I can't imagine what you felt … I mean … your mom. And you were just a kid … and your dad crying, didn't you say you'd never seen him cry before?

ANNA: Never before, never since. I just kept looking at him at the graveside, this strong man, you know, this strong, army man, the Colonel, displays of emotion antithetical to his being. And he was broken, completely broken. My Dad was so crippled with grief at the graveside and all I could think was that the way he was crying made me want to fall in love.

SCENE THREE
SEAN'S APARTMENT, NYC

SEAN on the telephone to his mother, LINDA. If we see LINDA she's far, far away and we should feel this.

LINDA: Describe the sky for me, Seany.

SEAN: The sky's black, Mum.

LINDA: Just black?

SEAN: A little grey, a little green even.

LINDA: Any clouds?

SEAN: It's too late at night for clouds.

LINDA: Is it? I get confused. Did I wake you up?

SEAN: No.

LINDA: Silly isn't it. After all these years I can't remember
    what time it is there, what time it is here. It's yesterday
    there, isn't it? My yesterday.

SEAN: That's right. It's Saturday. Saturday night.

LINDA: It's Sunday here. Worst day of the week, Sunday.
    They just drag on and on and

SEAN: I've been thinking …

LINDA: *(A joke.)* Don't do that, you'll hurt your head.

SEAN: You could start going to church again. The priest you
    saw, he's dead now. *(Beat.)* Mum?
    Claire told me. Two of us were thinking –

LINDA: You and your sister deciding what's best for me.
    Bit early for that don't you think? Senility hasn't hit yet.
    I don't piss and shit myself –

SEAN: Mum.

LINDA: Yet.

SEAN: There's a new priest now. You might like him. Or Claire could take you. *(Beat.)* Mum? *(Beat.)* Don't go quiet, Mum …

LINDA: Banished, Seany. I was banished.

SEAN: No …

LINDA: Yes, if you don't repent, you're banished. So I'm banished. That's that. Linda's not welcome in the house of God and Linda doesn't care because I know what I saw through the mist. God isn't good, Seany.

SEAN: The church is changing. It's in the papers all the time. The whole world is. Remember I told you about that woman I'm training? The fat, fat woman? Not fat any more. Lost eighty-five pounds. She cried! She didn't think it was possible. But change she did. We all have the potential for change.

LINDA: Says who? Where are you getting this stuff?

SEAN: I'm reading a book about it.

LINDA: What kind of book?

SEAN: It's about happiness.

LINDA: *(Sarcastic.)* You'll have to send me a copy.

SEAN: I will. It's a self-help book.

LINDA: A *what?* You've been living in America too long … You certainly are undergoing a process of change if you're reading a self-help book. *(Beat – then slightly anxious.)* What are you reading that for? *(Beat.)* Seany? *(Beat.)* Don't *you* go quiet … What are you reading a book about happiness for? Are you sad? Seany?

SEAN: I'm worried about you. Claire says you don't leave the house at all now.

LINDA: Let's not have a conversation with Claire in it, let's have a conversation that's just you and me, all by ourselves.

SEAN: Mum, you can't stay locked up in that house for the rest of your life!

LINDA: *(Beat.)* At night sometimes … I go to the window, and I open it a tiny little crack, and I listen.

SEAN: What do you hear?

LINDA: *Little* life. Insects and things. I think I'm a night creature. You were always a night creature. You used to be out on Saturday nights.

SEAN: *(Closing off, shutting down.)* I work on Saturdays now. I'm tired.

LINDA: What's the point of living in the big city if you don't go out on the town, Sean? That's what New York's *for*. Painting red. *(Beat.)* Are you lonely, Sean? *(Beat.)* I can hear you being lonely down the telephone. *(Beat.)* Is it that girl?

SEAN: *(Surprised.)* What girl?

LINDA: Rachel. You brought her home for a Christmas. She was Saturday nights. You'd come back sometimes and call me up, drunk and so happy, you were so full of love. You'd say "I love you, Mum. I love you so much …" and I could hear her laughing in the background and you sounded so happy, Sean.

SEAN: You know we broke up.

LINDA: Did she hurt you? Did she break your heart?

SEAN: I broke hers.

LINDA: *(Reassured.)* Oh well then … Looking for someone else, then, are you?

SEAN: Sure.

LINDA: What kind of person are you looking for?

SEAN: Someone who doesn't freebase.

LINDA: What?

SEAN: Nothing.

LINDA: You're not looking very hard if you're staying indoors on a Saturday night.

Pause.

SEAN: I'm just taking a break, Mum. I'll get back out there.

LINDA: *(Emphatically.)* You should do. You're too good to waste.

Beat.

SEAN: I have to put on my pajamas and go to bed. I have to be back at the gym at 6.30.

LINDA: If we stay on the phone just a little longer we'll be talking on the same day of the week. Shall we do that, Seany? Shall I describe the sky to you? Imagine a bucket of off-white paint. Do you see it?

SEAN: I do.

LINDA: Now stir in some black paint. Just a little bit. Stir it and stir it and stir it and stir it until it's nearly mixed through but not quite … that's what the sky looks like. Like dirty seagulls or dirty doves.

SEAN: I see it.

LINDA: I see yours. Black, green, like witches.

SEAN: Had a few drinks, have you?

LINDA: *(Distant.)* Oh who cares what I do with my time? It passes.

SCENE FOUR
COLUMBIA UNIVERSITY CAMPUS

ANNA and HELENA on a bench. Sandwiches. Spring. HELENA crying.

ANNA: I'm so sorry.

HELENA: That's what she said to me. "Maybe it's time for you to get another dog." In this like … bored tone. Like my grief is boring to her. Maybe it is. Maybe it's boring to you.

ANNA: It's not –

HELENA: It's boring to me actually. Feelings are boring. but they're *life*, what can you do? And my mother, my fucking mother, she thinks I should just buy another dog and magically …. And I get it. I mean it's been a year. It's just that she was all I had.

ANNA: That's not true.

HELENA: She's who I slept with every night. I mean she knew everything about me. Everything. She knew when I ate, when I cried, when I took a crap. And I loved her. It doesn't stop being real love just because it's a *dog*. I mean, if it had been another human being that I had lived with for fifteen years that suddenly died, if I had walked home and found a human being dead on the floor, lying in their own shit and piss with a look of pain, of twisted pain on their face, then a year later nobody would be surprised if I was still *upset*. Or would they? Who the fuck knows? People want other people to be perky.

ANNA: Look. Grief is hard. That's what love does to us. It hurts us, right?

HELENA: I don't think it's supposed to. Not always.

ANNA: Because of death, though. Love always hurts the one that's left behind.

HELENA: Right.

ANNA: You're supposed to grieve for something you loved.

HELENA hugs ANNA.

HELENA: Thank you for meeting me on your lunch break in the freezing cold!

ANNA gets a thick manuscript out of her bag.

15

HELENA: You'll think this is crazy but sometimes I can still feel Zoë with me …

ANNA: *(Ignoring that, passing the manuscript.)* You're the first person I've given this to.

HELENA: Is this …?

ANNA: I want to hear everything you have to say about it.

HELENA: "Keats' Punctuation"

ANNA: I need to find a snappier title. Any section you don't understand, I want to know about. Because I want it to be accessible, you know? And not just read by other Keats Scholars. I tried to make it … at least … the middle is kind of boring –

HELENA: Don't say that!

ANNA: But the beginning and the end … I tried to get to some place … human.

HELENA: You're so frikkin' incredible, you know that? I am so proud of you. You finished!

ANNA: It's just a first draft –

HELENA: It is a big deal. It is a big frikkin' deal.

They hug.

ANNA: I have to go teach. Don't you have to get back to work?

HELENA: No.

ANNA: How come?

HELENA: Because at five pm today, little ol' Helena has a little ol' audition.

ANNA: Oh that's great!

HELENA: Would you like to guess for what play?

ANNA: No.

HELENA: *A Midsummer Night's Dream.* Would you like to guess
for what part?

ANNA: I just don't have time.

HELENA: Helena! Isn't that crazy? Don't you think that *means*
something? That *her* name is already *my* name? I already
know what it's like to answer as Helena, I mean I know
that's superficial but ... I don't know. It feels meaningful to
me right now. And she's such a strong woman, you know?
That's how I see her. Strong. Guess where the production is?

ANNA: Where?

HELENA: Here! Columbia! A student production! Which is
great because that means it will really be about the work
and it just never is when you're trying to sell tickets, but
they don't sell tickets for student productions so ...

ANNA: Is it paid?

HELENA sighs. The sigh becomes a stony silence.

ANNA: I was just asking because if it's a graduate thesis
production they do pay the actors so –

HELENA: I don't know if it's paid.

ANNA: If it's not you can claim back on your tax return.
Call it an in-kind donation.

HELENA: Whatever. Maybe it's paid. Maybe it's not. I'd just
like to be working again. Not everything is about taxes,
Anna. I don't even do my taxes.

ANNA: Oh.

HELENA: I could hang around after my audition and we could
get a drink around here. I frikkin' miss student bars.

ANNA: I can't. I have a date.

HELENA: *(Disappointed.)* Who is it this time?

ANNA: A critic.

HELENA: *(Horrified.)* No …

ANNA: The machine kept matching me with lawyers and bankers. I adjusted my search criteria last week. Now it's matching me with journalists.

HELENA: You know Anna, the hunt for the soul mate, that is a mysterious thing, and I don't care how much you pay this website, the big old American dollar is not going to short cut that process. What if you're supposed to be with a coal miner or something? Or an acrobat? But the machine can't think out of the box, the machine keeps hooking you up with ivy league a-holes.

ANNA: It's my fault. Those are the guys I'm getting because those are the things I said were important to me. Education. Ambition. Money.

HELENA: You said money?

ANNA: Well … sure …

HELENA: *(Pure judgment.)* Wow.

ANNA: If this one's a disaster I'll change my search criteria.

HELENA: The very fact that there are criteria is a problem.

ANNA: An acrobat?

HELENA: I find it really offensive that you would go on a date with a critic. It's the equivalent of dating someone who's trying to kill me. *(Beat.)* Want to hear my audition speech?

ANNA: I have to go. Break a leg.

ANNA exits.

HELENA: Hey Anna!

"I am as ugly as a bear,
For beasts that meet me run away for fear …"

SCENE FIVE
LINDA'S HOUSE, IRELAND

Late at night. LINDA and MAX sit, drinks in hand, staring out into space.

LINDA: Sean's out tonight. Out on a date.

MAX: That's nice.

LINDA: A girl he met. On the internet.

MAX: On the internet?

LINDA: Not in a dirty way, in an organized way when they give details about the kind of person that they want to meet and –

MAX: I gotcha. Millie's cousin Marion was married that way.

LINDA: Really?

MAX: She was, she met a man through an internet website –

LINDA: That's it. It's a website –

MAX: Enthusiasts of cheese, I think it was –

LINDA: No this is different –

MAX: And they got along and within six months he'd popped the question. Now she's pregnant and they're talking about moving to Greece to set up a B&B.

LINDA: All Sean does now is go on dates.

MAX: Very nice.

LINDA: Tonight he dates a facialist.

MAX: What the fuck is a facialist?

LINDA: They squeeze your face and make it pretty.

MAX: *What?*

LINDA: That's what they do.

MAX: Why would squeezing your face make it pretty? It would make it blotchy I should think.

19

LINDA: Faces are full of pus.

MAX: Mine isn't.

LINDA: Everyone's is.

MAX: Mine isn't.

LINDA: Every time I talk to him he's going on a date. "Can't talk, Mum. Going on a date." "Getting ready for a date." "Out on a date." He is *obsessed* with the word date. I told him "only the people in the pictures go on dates." He took it the wrong way.

MAX: Kids *always* take things the wrong fucking way. You can't open your fucking mouth without them pointing out that you just *fucked* something for them. Like my girl, Janie. She's got emotional problems.

LINDA: Since when?

MAX: Since her *therapist* said so. And I swear to God, every single time I open my fucking mouth she says I'm belittling her. Every time I use the word "fucking" *she* says *he* says it's aggressive. So now I have to try and not use the word around her. And you know *why* she's got emotional problems? Do you know why every single kid in her generation has emotional problems?

LINDA: They're weak.

MAX: Their expectations are too fucking high! Animals are fucking happy. Not people.

LINDA: I kept Claire and Sean's expectations *very* low. They're happier as adults than they were as children, the only person they have to thank for that is me. There's nothing about it in the books, but there's something to be said for providing an upward trajectory.

MAX: Since Janie's been in counseling the only topic of conversation on offer is "remember when you broke my heart by not taking me fucking ice skating after you promised."

LINDA: Mine still criticize. Well, not Seany so much, course he's not here to criticize, but Claire ... "Remember the time," she'll say, "after Dad left and you didn't get out of bed for three days and I had to make the sandwiches?" *(Beat.)* What does she fucking want me to do about it *now*?

MAX: Stop saying "fucking!" You're emotionally damaging me!

LINDA: Claire's not making too good a parent herself. She dropped the baby the other day.

MAX: Whoops!

They roar with laughter. Pause.

MAX: Shouldn't criticize them. Not really.

LINDA: Why not? They sit around and complain about us.

MAX: I'm not saying I couldn't have done better. I'm not saying that. *(Beat.)* No, I am saying that. I will say that. I didn't drink much, worked hard, helped with homework, I mean what do they want? Jesus Christ could have fathered my Janie and she'd have said, "remember that time you were supposed to take me ice skating, but you had to go deal with the loaves and the fishes?" *(Beat.)* And the reason I didn't take her ice-skating was that I had band practice! Had to give it up in the end though, didn't I? And I don't call her up and say "remember when I gave up my rock band because there weren't enough hours in the day with everybody needing something from me! *(Beat.)* It's nice to be drunk. I haven't been drunk in a long time.

LINDA: Millie keeps you on a tight leash –

MAX: She made me promise I wouldn't get stinking. And I am stinking.

LINDA: What does she expect? You and I always got drunk together. Since we were kiddies.

MAX: You've drunk enough booze tonight to sink a bloody battleship.

LINDA: Bollocks. I can drink, and drink, and drink, and drink and it doesn't do a thing to me.

MAX: It's doing something to you, Linda. *(Beat.)* What time is it? I should call Millie.

He stands.

LINDA: Can't I have you to myself for one fucking night?

MAX: I was just going to go in the other room for a *second* ...

LINDA: Does Millie understand that you and I never see each other since she moved you to the other side of Ireland?

MAX: Linda, it will just take a minute.

LINDA: Oh a minute now, is it? First it was a second, then a minute, then you'll be gone for a full half hour, talking to another. *(Worked up.)* I see you once in a fucking blue moon and I can't have you all to myself for one night?

MAX: Ah, you're behaving badly now, that's the alcohol, that's what it's doing to you ... *(Beat. He thinks of a solution.)* I'll text her.

He gets out his phone. He inexpertly texts his wife.

MAX: Its probably better anyway. She'll only be cross at me for drinking.

LINDA: *(Fixing him with a stare.)* What are you telling her?

MAX: I'm writing that I love her.

LINDA rolls her eyes, but says nothing.

LINDA: Does Millie know? That tonight's the anniversary?

MAX: Of course.

LINDA: The anniversary of my death.

MAX: Don't say that.

LINDA: My ending, the termination of little Linda was twenty-one years ago tonight. And back then she was pretty as picture. Remember her? A young thing in a yellow dress. And then boom! As old as the cliffs. *(Beat.)* And where's he tonight I wonder?

MAX: Who?

LINDA: The man in the mist. At home with his family? Playing with his children?

MAX claps his hands.

MAX: Don't get maudlin.

LINDA: Get what?

MAX: Maudlin.

LINDA: I don't even know what that means.

MAX: Mournful. Morbid. Melancholy.

LINDA: How'd you ever hear a word like that?

MAX: It's just a word.

LINDA: Think I'm stupid now, do you?

MAX: No.

LINDA: Maudlin. I'm entitled to be maudlin, I think. Tonight. Do you mind if I'm maudlin for one fucking night? I never *tell* anyone how I feel! I never talk about the nightmares! I never repeat what plays round and around in my head. It's a lot of fucking energy to stay silent Max! Can I indulge myself a little tonight? On the fucking anniversary!

Beat.

MAX: Say whatever you want, Linda.

LINDA: I want to die ... I want to be dead ...

MAX: Always?

LINDA: I don't know.

MAX: I know I made fun of the counseling before but ... for you it's different. It's deserved ... I could pay if you'd like to see a person who is trained in ... your pain, Linda.

LINDA: I don't think ... I don't think ....I can do it. I had the counseling at the time and it didn't ... *(Distress, panic.)* I'm too sad. Everybody says. It's why Martin left. He'd come home, I'd be staring into space. "I'm so sorry, Martin," I'd say. "I'll get myself together." "Don't worry," he'd say. "You're entitled." But I never let him touch me again, and then he was gone.

MAX: Martin was a bastard.

LINDA: Cost me my husband, that man in the mist. And then my son.

MAX: No ...

LINDA: He's why Sean left! Now he's out on a date! He'll marry out there and never come back!

MAX: He's a young man, Linda! That's what young men do! They go out in the world! They seek adventure!

LINDA: All the tiny little stones I picked from his tiny little cuts on his tiny little knees and he's gone. Bought a pair of long trousers and off he went across the sea, not a look over his shoulder not a word of apology. You spend every last pence you have on them! The constant buying of things for children! The T-Shirts and posters and key rings, pound after pound after pound and then boom! Grown men and women and you're at their mercy! I wish I hadn't come back! I wish I had jumped! The man in the mist had killed me so what was the fucking point!

MAX: Linda, you wanted to live. You want to live ...

LINDA: *(In pieces.)* I'm sorry, Max! I know this must be awful for you!

MAX: *(Grim.)* You're my sister. It's the least I can fucking do.

SCENE SIX
KAY'S HOUSE, DC

KAY wears pajamas.

KAY: What the hell are you doing here, Colonel? You're supposed to be in New York.

ADAM: Surprise?

KAY: You're supposed to be spending the night at Anna's.

ADAM: Surprise.

KAY: You said you weren't coming to DC until tomorrow.

ADAM: It is tomorrow.

KAY: It's 4am!

ADAM: I'm just a little early.

KAY: Something's wrong. I swear to God, I don't see you from one year to the next then you show up like a bad penny and spill your guts.

ADAM: I thought it would be like the old days in Texas. Me knocking your door in the middle of the night, hoping for …

KAY: *(Playful.)* Hoping for what?

ADAM: Hoping to see you.

KAY: Give me a kiss.

ADAM looks around him. The room is mostly bare.

ADAM: What happened here?

KAY: Everything's in storage. I told you on the phone.
  I'm taking a trip.

ADAM: For how long?

KAY: A while.

ADAM: You're renting the place out?

KAY: Selling.

ADAM: Where do you plan on living when you get home?

KAY: I haven't made any definite plans.

ADAM: Why haven't you made any definite plans?

KAY: Because it's liberating.

ADAM: Just how sick are you?

Pause. ADAM continues to study the empty space.

KAY: You were going to have a drink in your hand when
  I told you. *(Beat.)* I have defeated Western Medicine.
  So I'm headed east. To India. I shall see mystical people.
  Maybe they'll wave their hands over me and make it all
  go away.

ADAM starts to ask another question.

KAY: And then I was going to tell you that I don't want to
  talk about it any more. It's not my favorite subject.

Beat. ADAM nods.

ADAM: I shouldn't have woken you up.

KAY: But you did so why don't you tell me what's wrong?
  Why didn't you stay at Anna's?

ADAM: It's not important any more.

KAY: Of course it is.

ADAM: Forget it.

Beat.

KAY: So how is Anna?

ADAM: Good.

KAY: Last time I saw you she was at Columbia, right?

ADAM: She's teaching there now. Got her PhD.

KAY: *Dr* Anna.

ADAM: She's writing a book.

KAY: What's it about?

ADAM: Nothing. Punctuation. She's been telling me about the damn thing for years, I have no idea what she's talking about.

KAY: Punctuation's important.

ADAM: Is it?

KAY: Sure. Without it nothing would make any sense. Period.

ADAM: Our conversations are a blast. She tells me about her work which I don't understand and I can't tell her about my work because it's classified.

KAY: *(Beat.)* Is she seeing anyone?

ADAM sighs.

KAY: Aha. Who?

ADAM: A personal trainer. What kind of job *is* that?

KAY: Fitness and such. The two of you probably have a lot in common.

ADAM: I am a colonel in the United States Armed Forces, Kay. I am not a fitness instructor.

KAY: *(Amused.)* Sorry.

ADAM: She brought him to dinner! No warning, just brought him to dinner. I mean, maybe I wouldn't have minded so much if this guy had anything to recommend him, you know. He didn't even tuck his shirt in. He's Irish.

KAY: Sexy.

ADAM: I'm not one of those Americans who's sappy about Ireland. *(Beat.)* I asked if he planned to go back, he didn't even answer. He just shrugged. Language is not his first language if you know what I mean.

KAY: Maybe he was shy.

ADAM: His father's dead. His mother … I could not get a clear picture of the mother. I did gather that she was unemployed.

KAY: Adam. Honey. You're not supposed to like him. He's screwing your daughter. *(Beat.)* Has she ever brought any other boy to dinner?

ADAM: No.

KAY: So this one's important.

ADAM: They were clamped together at this restaurant. Physically clamped. Finally, he goes to the bathroom and she says "for the first time I really understand what you and Mom had."

KAY: Oh boy.

ADAM: And she's glowing, you know? Just glowing. I felt sick.

KAY: Adam …

ADAM: We're strangers! She put her hand on my arm, looked into my eyes, and she was a stranger. And then the personal trainer came back from the bathroom, sat down, stuck his arm around her like she was his property, and I picked up the check.

KAY: Adam …

ADAM: I could hear my dead wife laughing.

KAY: What was she finding so funny.

ADAM: She told me this would happen! "Some day that little
girl will be all grown up and you'll have missed her."
And she was right. Good for Rosie.

KAY: Adam … It's not too late.

ADAM: Oh I think it is. I've always known that Anna and
I had to struggle for conversation a little, I didn't mind.
When it was just Anna and me we were both outsiders,
you know? Trying to get in. But Anna and another … that
makes me the outsider. That makes *me* the stranger. *(Beat.)*
On the way here I kept thinking "I should feel young
again. Finally, no dependents." But I swear to God I feel a
thousand years old.

KAY: You're not a thousand years old, you're a thousand
different ages. We all are. Right now you look just the same
as when we first met. A frightened man in his twenties.

ADAM: You're hallucinating. What kind of drugs have they got
you on anyway?

KAY: You were running from Anna just like now. You said you
needed a break from the screaming. I said "Colonel, you're
hilarious. Your country needs you and you shoulder the
burden. Your family needs you and you head to the nearest
bar."

ADAM: *(Irritated.)* Look, don't blame me, Kay. I make the
effort. What the hell do you think these dinners are about?
Why the hell do you think I fly in to New York every time
I have to report to DC even though I hate New York!
She hates Texas so I never ask her to come to Texas.
It's me that makes the effort! I have been making the effort
for years! I show up at the over priced hell-hole that she's
picked and I sit there!

Beat.

KAY: Don't show up at four in the morning, ask for my help and then yell at me. I am not a wife. *(Beat.)* It's not too late.

ADAM: It is too late. Rosie was right. I missed her. She passed me by.

KAY: If she passed you by, you know what to do.

ADAM: No. I don't.

KAY: For God's sakes man, give chase!

SCENE SEVEN
AN ART GALLERY

ANNA and HELENA staring at incomprehensibly abstract modern art. Eventually HELENA begins to study ANNA instead.

HELENA: Miss Anna? You are totally wearing a little outfit.

ANNA: What do you mean?

HELENA: You're wearing a little scarf.

ANNA: So?

HELENA: Your bag matches your shoes.

ANNA: Are you complimenting me?

HELENA: I am complimenting you, absolutely I am. You look incredible.

ANNA: Thanks.

HELENA: When did you become such a *woman*? When did you become such an adult lady? I mean maybe that it's that I haven't seen you in a while but you look so different. I mean you always look beautiful but right now what I'm getting, what you're projecting, what I'm picking up, is that you are an adult suddenly. You look great. You look really put together.

ANNA: Thanks.

HELENA: You look like the kind of lady I have no business knowing. You look like the kind of lady who has stocks.

ANNA: I do have some stocks.

HELENA: *(Flabbergasted.)* From the stock market? Shares? You have shares in things?

ANNA: Sure.

HELENA: What stocks do you have?

ANNA: Most of it's in environmentally friendly waste management.

HELENA: Wow. I am a child. Do you think I'm like a child?

ANNA: No.

HELENA: Really? Even though I dress like a clown?

ANNA: I like how you dress.

HELENA: I'm just so used to seeing you in jeans. Where did these dresses come from all of a sudden. Is it Sean? Does he prefer you in dresses?

ANNA: He's never commented one way or the other.

HELENA: Oh really? He doesn't care what you wear?

ANNA: I don't think so.

HELENA: That's nice. It's so long since I've been in a relationship that I can't remember what it's like. Somehow, in my imagination, the guy says "you must wear *this,* woman! Now suck my cock!" but that's not what it's like, right? That's just my fucked up imagination. Honestly, secretly, I think I'm terrified of men. Even like, with my brother sometimes, he'll be talking to me and all I'll be thinking is "you have a penis, you have a penis" and I find it *terrifying.* You know what I mean?

ANNA: Kind of …

HELENA: No but it's so great about you and Sean. You seem so happy.

ANNA: I am.

HELENA: That's great. Isn't it amazing how we find each other? Like him being Irish and a personal trainer, I mean, that's crazy! He's from Ireland!

ANNA: I know.

HELENA: And a personal trainer! I would never have thought in a million years that you – or in fact anyone I know – could find a meaningful relationship with a personal trainer. But you have. *(Beat.)* Do you guys have sex all the time?

ANNA: No.

HELENA: And you said it was really good, right. You said the sex was good.

ANNA: Sure.

HELENA: Can you see me with a boyfriend? Can you see that in my future?

ANNA: Of course.

HELENA: That's good. Sometimes I find I can't … *(Her voice starts to break a little, tears close.)* picture it as closely as I used to. The only guys that like me are married, or gay. The last time little Helena actually had full blown sex, it turned out the guy was married. Anyhow, let's talk about you, we always talk about me, let's talk about you. You want to?

ANNA: Sure …

HELENA: Talk. I'll listen.

ANNA: Something weird happened last night. My Dad telephoned. Just, he said, to *chat*. I have never heard him use the word chat in his life.

HELENA: Right, you guys don't chat, you have awkward conversations twice a year.

ANNA: Exactly.

HELENA: So how was chatting?

ANNA: It was ridiculous. We have nothing to chat about. Normally I hide that by never shutting up. I saw a fascinating movie I say, I'll say. A student came to me with a fascinating problem. I'm always trying to fascinate him. And I don't think I've ever fascinated him once.

HELENA: God that's so sad.

ANNA: I know. All I do is try to entertain him.

HELENA: Like a geisha.

ANNA: Right. But on the phone, last night, I didn't. There was a lot of silence. *(Beat.)* I didn't tell him the big news.

HELENA: What's the big news?

ANNA: Another publisher passed on my book.

HELENA: *What?* What is wrong with these people?

ANNA: Nobody is interested in Keats' Punctuation. I should have seen that coming, really. I mean I wasn't even interested half the time I was writing it, I wanted to write about Emily Dickenson's punctuation, remember, but then Simon said everyone wrote about Emily Dickenson's punctuation and I just happened to be reading Keats at the time, and now it's five fucking years later and my whole life has been about Keats's punctuation and it looks like it was a waste of time.

HELENA: If no one wants to publish your book that just confirms that it's frikkin' excellent. It's a topsy-turvy universe. If something is worthless, we raise it up. Something of value, we trample it into the frikkin' mud.

ANNA: It's the title, Sean thinks. It's the fucking title. "Keats' Punctuation."

HELENA: Did Sean also tell you that you're a genius and that your book is brilliant?

ANNA: He hasn't read it.

HELENA: What?

ANNA: I told him not to. It would bore him.

HELENA: But you wrote it.

ANNA: But it's not for everybody. Which is why they won't publish it. *(Beat.)* What?

HELENA: I just don't see how you can be with someone who doesn't want to read your work.

ANNA: He read a chapter, I think.

HELENA: *(Shocked.)* How could he only read a chapter of it? It's your brain, it's your heart, it's your soul, how can he – I don't even *know* Sean. I find it really weird that you've been seeing each other forever and I've met him like five times. Does he even like me?

ANNA: Of course he does.

HELENA: Because I kind of got the impression that he didn't like me.

ANNA: When?

HELENA: You remember how I was telling the story about how I got really drunk at my dad's sixtieth birthday party and cried and kind of ruined it for everybody and he just seemed really judgmental.

ANNA: I don't think he was judging you. He was just listening.

HELENA: Even you said he was judgmental, remember. Didn't you tell me that on your first date he totally judged you for being in therapy?

ANNA: I was wrong. That was – that was about something else.

HELENA: You never tell me anything about him.

ANNA: What is it that you want to know?

HELENA: I don't *know*, you just never talk about him.

ANNA: Because there's nothing to say.

HELENA: That can't be true. He's such a huge part of your life! And I totally feel you making him separate!

ANNA: I'm not.

HELENA: Yes you *are!*

ANNA: He works all the time. I work all the time. The little time we have together we want to spend by ourselves. And if I don't talk about him it's because I have nothing to say about him except that I *love* him. And he makes me happy. And it makes you unhappy when I'm happy.

HELENA: I can't believe you would think that.

ANNA: We start talking about me being happy and within ten minutes you're in tears because you're not happy as well. You and me like to talk about our problems. Sean's not a problem so I don't want to talk about him. No one wants to publish my fucking book, let's talk about that. My Dad is calling me on the phone and acting crazy, let's talk about that! This exhibition is horrifying, let's talk about that. But leave Sean alone!

HELENA: Wow. I had no idea you felt this way. Thank you for telling me. This is very enlightening.

Pause.

HELENA: Maybe I do cry a lot because guess what, big surprise, little ol' Helena is an emotional person, – but I think I am also a very joyful person –

ANNA: You are …

HELENA: I am a person of extremes, but do not tell me that I am incapable of celebrating with you. Do not tell me I am the person who can only discuss misery.

ANNA: Not just miserable things. Deep things! Like ... art ... and ... you know ... Deep things!

HELENA: But you're in love, Anna! Isn't love deep?

ANNA: It's private. It's private right now.

Pause.

HELENA: But you're happy. And the sex is wonderful.

ANNA: Sometimes we have sex and it's wonderful. Sometimes I never felt more alone in my life.

SCENE EIGHT
A GYM, DUBLIN, IRELAND

MAX, sweating, exhausted, is on the running machine. SEAN stands next to him.

MAX: This woman you're seeing ...

SEAN: Anna.

MAX: Do you torture her like this?

SEAN: She has no interest.

MAX: Been going on for sometime now, hasn't it? *(No response from SEAN.)* When are we going to meet her? Does she not want to visit this marvelous country of ours?

SEAN: Oh she does. Very much.

MAX: So?

SEAN: I'll never bring a girl home again unless it's to ask her to marry me.

MAX: It must be about that time, isn't right?

SEAN: According to who's timetable?

MAX: Well how serious is it? What are you doing?

SEAN speeds up the machine. MAX runs.

MAX: Isn't this just a metaphor for life? You sweat and you strain and you still end up in the same place. This is giving me an existential crisis! *(Running faster.)* You're a fucking torturer. I had no idea. I had no idea that torturing people was your fucking career of choice ... Vanity. One of the seven deadly sins. A man my age is supposed to spread a little.

SEAN: You'd find this easier if you would just shut up.

MAX: I think I might die. Soon. In the next five minutes. I feel it. My death approaches. He's at my back. You're killing your uncle, Sean. You're own flesh and blood. This can't be healthy.

SEAN: It is.

MAX: But I'm about to throw up.

SEAN: You're doing great.

MAX: Oh you're just feeding me your personal trainer bullshit. I'm not an American, Sean. I don't believe I'm the best fucker in the world just because somebody tells me so!

SEAN: Alright, what about this. You're a heart attack waiting to happen! And when you're dead Auntie Millie will say "that lazy bastard. I could have had him for another fifteen years if only he exercised more."

MAX: Fifteen years?

SEAN: Now you know what you're chasing after.

Pause. MAX runs, more determined.

SEAN: A few more seconds now ...

MAX: Fuck you! This is bullshit! This is a terrible way to spend time!

SEAN: Ten, nine, eight, seven ...

MAX: I hate you Sean, I hate you Sean!

SEAN: Five, four …

MAX: Fuck you! Fuck me! Fuck everybody!

SEAN: And now we slow down to walking …

SEAN slows the machine down to a fast walk.

MAX: We don't stop?

SEAN: No. We get our heart rate down, we get our breath back, but we keep going …

MAX: "We" nothing! What are you doing? You get paid for this shit?

SEAN: I do.

MAX: I'm going to be in pain tomorrow, aren't I? This is the last walking I'll be doing for quite some time, isn't that right?

SEAN: Got to push through the pain, Max.

MAX: Listen to you … like a fucking Marine …

SEAN: You're doing great.

MAX: I am not doing great! I am pathetic. The seventeen-year-old Max is watching and he is in tears.

SEAN: You really are doing well.

MAX: What happened to great? *(His breath is steadier now.)* So this girl you've been seeing. We were talking about whether or not it was serious.

SEAN: Her name is Anna.

MAX: Well, you're on the other side of the world, Sean! We've never met her! She's not quite real to us, you know what I mean? You're mother's worried you're keeping her away deliberately.

SEAN: Why?

MAX: She thinks you're ashamed of where you're from.

SEAN: That's ridiculous.

MAX: She gets the impression that Anna is a different sort of person, a posh sort of person. Teaches at a university, doesn't she? Your mother would feel better if she met her, that's all. But if it's not going to last –

SEAN: I didn't say it wasn't going to last.

MAX: Well two years, boy! When I was your age I had two kids already! The time goes by quick, what are you waiting for? A sign from God? If she's not the right fish throw her back in the sea.

SEAN: How do I know?

MAX: How do you know? Do you love her?

SEAN: Aye.

MAX: No but do you really love her, do you truly love her? No, don't make me run!

But SEAN has stopped the machine. MAX sees SEAN looks very serious.

What? What's the matter with you? *(A beat.)* What Sean?

SEAN: I don't know. She wants to move in together. I don't want to. And if I don't want to then I should end it. But I don't want to end it. I'm a dick. I don't know what I'm doing. She probably wants to have babies. And I'm just … I don't know what to do! I don't want to be the bad guy! But I don't want to end it! But I *should* end it because I'm a liar!

MAX: Who are you lying to?

SEAN: To Anna! I'm lying next to her at night and against my will against my fucking will there's this other girl in my head and I'm thinking that I love her. Or that I loved her. I loved her more.

MAX: Who?

SEAN: Rachel. *(Beat.)* Christ, Max. I'm asleep with one woman I'm dreaming of another.

MAX: I haven't done enough for you, Sean. You had no Dad and I've tried to look out for you but with four of my own and …

SEAN: Max –

MAX: Let me finish. I've been remiss in my responsibilities towards you. A kid needs a father. You need a father, this moment right here is why a child needs a father. Let me be yours. For this moment, let me be yours.

SEAN: Alright.

MAX: Son. You will always think of other women. *(Beat.)* I do, even now. Helen May.

SEAN: You've not been remiss, Max. You had your own family.

MAX: But you are my family.

SEAN: I'm alright.

MAX: I don't know how you did it, but you've grown up fine.

Beat.

SEAN: So who was Helen May then?

MAX: It was with her that I had my first kiss. Beautiful girl. Became a nun.

SEAN: I see you had quite an effect on her.

MAX: We were kids. Running around the playground. The girls would make daisy chains and chase the boys. If they put the chain around their necks they had to kiss them. And us boys off we ran. We ran, but we wanted to be caught. Helen May caught me. So we turned and we faced each other. And I bent forward like I was bowing, you know? And we were making these little Chinese bows at each other. And I closed my eyes and she kissed me. Oh it was delicious. Some nights, Millie is asleep, and I pretend

that I seek out Helen May in her nunnery. I call up to the
tower! Helen, do you remember me? Run away with me!
Millie gives a little snort and awakes. "I can't sleep," I tell
her. "Well think about Helen May," she says. "That usually
drops you off." *(Beat.)*

SEAN: *(Surprised.)* She doesn't mind it?

MAX: She doesn't mind.

SCENE NINE
LECTURE THEATER, COLUMBIA UNIVERSITY

*ADAM alone. Awkward. Out of place. The outskirts of a party. HELENA
arrives, hurried. She looks disheveled. ADAM is relieved to see someone
he knows.*

ADAM: Helena!

HELENA: Hey … how are you? Gosh it's been ….

ADAM: A long time.

HELENA: Can you believe it? She's totally published!
Awesome! Where is she?

ADAM nods off stage.

HELENA: The woman of the hour.

ADAM: I'm just letting her do her thing.

HELENA: How long are you in town for?

ADAM: Just a couple of hours. The timing was off for me.

HELENA: That's so amazing that you flew in!

ADAM: Wouldn't miss it.

HELENA: I'm late-a-roony. I decided to have a catnap and it
turned into a sleeporama. I have very vivid dreams, you
know, and I was just having this crazy dream that I –

SEAN comes over.

SEAN: Helena. How are you?

HELENA: Honestly, I hate being asked that. People just want you to say fine. It's a lot of pressure. There's so much pressure to be *unreal* with people, you know?

SEAN: OK …

HELENA: OK.

SEAN: *(To ADAM.)* Anna told me to check on you. She's in the middle of a very dry conversation about ellipses.

HELENA: Ellipses are fascinating, actually.

ADAM: I don't even know what they are.

HELENA: They're the little dot dot dot at the end of a sentence. They change everything. For actors.

ADAM: Helena, what are you working on now?

A long pause. Gradually it dawns on ADAM that HELENA will not be answering his question.

HELENA: Is there any wine at this shindig?

SEAN: Over there.

HELENA exits towards wine. Pause.

SEAN: Work going well for you, Adam?

ADAM: Very well. *(Beat.)* And yours? Work?

SEAN: Great. Fine. *(Beat.)* I've been taking a class in Karate. I might incorporate it into some of the training.

ADAM: I have a black belt in Karate.

SEAN: Anna told me. You could give me a few pointers, maybe.

ADAM: When I was taught the object was to kill the other person. Different kind of training.

The ensuing silence is broken by the SCREETCH of a microphone.
Then we hear SIMON's amplified voice. All our attention is on ADAM
and SEAN's reactions.

SIMON: *(Offstage.)* Welcome everybody, welcome. I won't take
up much of your time I just want to say how pleased we are
to host this event tonight. Anna –

ADAM and SEAN listen, pride on their faces.

SIMON: – began life as an undergrad here at Columbia.
No actually, she began life as a baby. My little joke. Sorry.

ADAM and SEAN are unimpressed.

SIMON: *(Offstage.)* Anna began her *academic* life at Columbia
as an undergraduate and I actually had the pleasure of
teaching her … she was everything you want a student to
be, quick, attentive, studious, curious, passionate.

Pride on ADAM and SEAN's face. They even smile at each other.

SIMON: *(Offstage.)* Anna went on to get her PhD here, and to
my great delight she and I became more than student and
teacher …

ADAM and SEAN tense, horrified.

… we became colleagues.

ADAM and SEAN relax.

SIMON: *(Offstage.)* Tonight, we are here to celebrate the book
that bloomed from her PhD thesis. *The Grammar of Love:*
Keats and Punctuation represents Anna's first academic
publication. It's really wonderful and without a doubt
one of the most exciting publications to have come out of
Columbia all *year*. So, Anna, if you'd like to come up here
and say a few words?

HELENA walks up to ADAM and SEAN. We hear ANNA's voice
through the microphone.

ANNA: Thanks everyone for coming ... I want to thank Simon especially for so much help with the book and the faculty for all of their support and my dad for flying all the way in from Texas and my boyfriend for putting up with me and ... you know ... thanks for coming ...! Drink up!

SCREETCH. The microphone is switched off. ADAM and SEAN are modestly delighted with their acknowledgement.

SEAN: *(To HELENA.)* After this, I thought we'd get a drink downtown. I hate student bars.

ADAM: Anna's mother would have been incredibly proud of her. She always hoped to write a book herself.

HELENA: Everyone has a novel in them, right?

ADAM: She never had the discipline to get it out.

ANNA enters.

ANNA: *(Tense.)* That was a horrible speech.

SEAN: No.

ADAM: Short, quick and to the point.

SEAN: You thanked everyone you needed to thank and then you got off the stage.

HELENA bursts into tears and runs off stage.

ADAM: What's the matter with her?

SEAN: This isn't about the dog again, is it?

ADAM: The what?

SEAN: Her dog died a hundred years ago. She's still in mourning.

ANNA: It's because I didn't thank her. She read the book three times and I didn't thank her. I should have thanked her ...

SEAN: That's ridiculous.

ANNA: I meant to I just, I was flustered.

SEAN: You've thanked her *in* the book. It's fine.

ANNA: That's why she's crying. Bet you.

SEAN: *(Angry.)* Then she can get over it. Jesus, it's your night.

ANNA: Some night. Could it be any more anti-climactic? Five years of work and this is what I get? Wine, cheese, and a lecture theatre. There's still equations left up on the blackboard for fuck's sake. Sorry, Dad.

ADAM: Come now. *(Beat.)* Come now.

ANNA: Yeah, well now I have to write another one. It never ends. *(Beat.)* I better see if Helena's alright –

SEAN: *Leave* her … It's your night.

Beat.

ANNA: *(To SEAN.)* I am so fucking sick of her – *(To ADAM.)* sorry Dad – *(To SEAN.)* I swear to God it's the one night that's meant to be about me and she dragged me to one side and started telling me her dream, and when the head of the faculty came over to introduce me to some donor or something, she acted really … you know … mad. Like she was mad that the story of her *dream* got interrupted. I mean for God sakes …

ADAM: *(Emphatically.)* She has *aged.* I almost didn't recognize her. How's her acting going?

SEAN: She never works.

ADAM: Didn't you take me to see a play she was in?

ANNA: Ages ago.

ADAM: I thought she was *excellent.*

ANNA: She was.

ADAM: *Really* talented, I thought.

ANNA: What time's your flight?

ADAM: I've got about an hour still.

ANNA: You should go now. Get some food. You can't eat cheese for dinner. I have to stay for the end. I'm sorry it's such a pathetic little gathering, Dad. I told you it wasn't worth flying in for. Oh Jesus, I'm being waved over. *(To SEAN.)* Come with.

They walk off. ADAM alone. He's almost relieved to see a tear stained HELENA.

ADAM: Are you OK?

HELENA: Oh fine. I cry all the time. *(Beat.)* You know, I just woke up I had a really intense dream so …

ADAM: I just remembered. Last time I saw you I was here. You were doing a show with the students.

HELENA: *A Midsummer Night's Dream.*

ADAM: That's right! You played Bottom!

HELENA: Right …

ADAM: You were excellent. *(Beat.)* I have to go. It was good to see you, Helena.

He leaves.

HELENA: *(To the audience.)* I had this dream that I passed a store front and there were jellos in the window. I went inside. There was a back room full of children. My Dad was there. He was playing with them. I said surprised, "What are you doing here, Dad?" He was confused, like he didn't understand the question. He was playing cards with a little girl so I let him be. I started talking to a serious little boy. The boy told me he'd tried to kill himself that morning. He told me all the children there had tried to die. And then I remembered that I had tried to kill myself the day before. That's why my Dad was there. He was there for me.

SCENE TEN
ACADIA NATIONAL PARK, MAINE

SEAN and RACHEL sitting on a bench. A cold, blowy day.

RACHEL: Smoke?

SEAN: Gave up.

RACHEL: You always were a goody two shoes.

SEAN: Set a good example for my clients. You know.

RACHEL: How'd you find me?

SEAN: Facebook.

RACHEL: You're not on Facebook.

SEAN: I had to join it to find you.

RACHEL: I looked for you there when I joined. But I figured it wasn't very you.

SEAN: So you didn't mind me getting in touch?

RACHEL: No, why should I?

SEAN: Never pegged you for a country girl.

RACHEL: I'm not really.

SEAN: You're married.

RACHEL: Yes.

SEAN: Not a question. Facebook. Tells you everything, really. So much stuff. I had no idea. I had no idea. Ten minutes after I joined three ex-girlfriends in Ireland wanted to know what I was up to. Sending me quizzes to find out which golden girl I'm most like. *(Beat.)* Rose by the way. *(Beat.)* I shut my page down already. *(Beat.)* Anyway, sorry, Who'd you marry?

RACHEL: His name's Devrak.

SEAN: What is it?

RACHEL: Devrak. He's from India.

SEAN: I didn't know there were Indian people in Maine.

RACHEL: Had you ever seriously thought about it?

SEAN: No.

RACHEL: What about you? Married? Girlfriend?

SEAN: Girlfriend.

RACHEL: What's her name?

SEAN: Anna.

RACHEL: Serious?

SEAN: Yup.

RACHEL: Where are you working now?

SEAN: Freelance now.

RACHEL: Still saving to run your own gym?

SEAN: Yes.

RACHEL: You always said it would take years.

SEAN: I was right.

RACHEL: I'm a – oh you already know … Facebook.

SEAN: You're a hairdresser.

RACHEL: Stylist.

SEAN: You never did go back to school then?

RACHEL: No. *(Beat.)* I like cutting hair. I don't talk enough. My boss always tells me to be more chatty. But my regulars, that's what they like about me.

SEAN: That's funny.

RACHEL: What is?

SEAN: That's what my boss used to tell me. That's what I'd tell him.

RACHEL: I think that's why we liked to drink so much together. Loosened our lips.

SEAN: I drink less now.

RACHEL: I was AA all the way, baby. AA. I don't miss any of it. Half the people in my band are in recovery.

SEAN: *(Pleased.)* You're still playing?

RACHEL: Oh yes. We have kind of a following here in Maine. We're what they call "Maimous."

SEAN: How are your parents?

RACHEL: Good. Very good. Retired. I don't know where they are half the time. They bought an RV, travel up and down the country.

SEAN: I remember them saying they'd do that someday.

RACHEL: Some day's here.

Pause. SEAN begins to cry.

SEAN: I miss you. I still miss you. It doesn't go away. Don't say anything back. The last time I saw you, you had tubes coming out of your fucking nose. There were fucking sirens.

RACHEL: I'm sorry.

SEAN: *(Getting himself back together.)* I hate the sound of sirens. Can't stand hospitals. You know who else I think of all the time? Your folks. They hate my guts, I bet.

RACHEL: They don't think about you.

SEAN: I'll never forget your Dad screaming at me in the hospital. He hit me. Did you know that? Or tried to. I jumped back. I wish I hadn't now. I wish he'd hit me hard in the face, sometimes I pretend he did. If I can't sleep, I imagine him hitting me again and again.

RACHEL: He shouldn't have done that. It wasn't your fault. You had every right to dump me.

SEAN: Dump you, hook up with you, dump you, hook up with you, and on and on and on ... I was a fucking idiot.

RACHEL: Young love. That's what it looks like.

SEAN: I'm so sorry about it.

RACHEL: You don't need to be. It really had nothing to do with you.

SEAN: Oh please –

RACHEL: It didn't. It had to do with me. Honey, back then I was drinking a bottle of vodka a day.

SEAN: I didn't know that.

RACHEL: Well I was. I was a time-bomb. That's what my lady said.

SEAN: Your what?

RACHEL: They make you see a shrink if you try to kill yourself. I was a train wreck back then.

SEAN: Not to me.

RACHEL: Yes to you. That's why you kept dumping me!

SEAN: I don't remember. I don't remember why I broke it off. I keep asking myself why.

RACHEL: What you said was ... we need to grow up.

Pause.

RACHEL: Does your girlfriend know you came?

SEAN: Her suggestion. She said – she kept using this stupid word.

RACHEL: What word?

SEAN: It doesn't matter. It's silly.

RACHEL: What word?

SEAN: Traumatized.

Pause.

SEAN: What did your lady say about me?

RACHEL: Not much. We talked about my family mostly.

SEAN: Oh.

Pause.

RACHEL: But she said when I think of you, and I do think of you, it's just a fantasy of escape. The Sean I think of doesn't exist anymore. He's gone. And the Rachel you're thinking of doesn't exist either. Not really. She's long gone.

Pause.

SEAN: I don't exist?

RACHEL: Neither do I.

SCENE ELEVEN
ADAM'S HOUSE, TEXAS

Christmas Eve. ANNA holds a notebook. ADAM studies her. Very anxious.

ADAM: I don't know what to say. Do you want to call Sean? What can I do? Anna? I don't know what to say …

ANNA hurls the notebook at ADAM who has to dodge to avoid it.

ANNA: You can stop staying *that!*

ADAM: Hey!

ANNA: Asshole!

ADAM: Do you want to call Sean?

ANNA: Why would I want to call Sean?

ADAM: To comfort you …

ANNA: God I hate you! I have worked so hard not to hate you and now I give up. I hate you.

ADAM: I haven't done anything! I didn't even know she kept a journal!

ANNA: Of course not! Apparently you paid her no attention at all!

ADAM: I don't know what she wrote in there, but obviously it's just one half of the truth. The truth exists between two opposing viewpoints, don't forget that, don't ever forget that.

ANNA: Patronizing. She said you were patronizing. She captured you perfectly. And I've been ignoring –

ADAM: What? No –

ANNA: – Ignoring who you really were because I thought it was her, that it was her death that made you –

ADAM: Anna …

ANNA: She hated you!

ADAM: No! Not always.

ANNA: And you let me believe that it was a love story!

ADAM: It was! It … Anna you're not …

ANNA: What?

ADAM: *(Angry.)* Will you let me think? Will you just let me think? *(Beat.)* I have sensed from you a misunderstanding about the nature of the marriage for some time now and … *You* tell me how I was supposed to *correct* something like that? You got it all built up in your head. Not to blame you, not to blame you, but you must see that … Anna, every couple has their problems, you're a big girl now, you know that. I'm sure you and Sean have your problems, it doesn't mean … Please don't be so upset … Jesus Christ, Anna! I didn't know it was up there! I kept all her things in case you wanted to go through them some day! If I thought there was anything in there that would have upset you, I would have burned it! As would she! *(Uselessly completing his sentence.)* Have ... I know she wasn't happy. There was a period where she was not happy. Neither was I. Is that what upsets you? What did she write? How unhappy was she?

ANNA: Read it!

ADAM: Anna it was a different time, it was a difficult time, men and women spoke to each other in different ways. Anna will you look at me, please? Let's talk about this. I don't want this to ... please do not let this ... I have been trying very hard to ....It's Christmas Eve. Come on now. This is our first Christmas together for a long time, and it's supposed to be ... we were having a very nice time I thought ... and Sean is flying in for New Year. This is supposed to be a new fucking era or whatever. Jesus! Why is it always like this! Why is it always such a fucking drama?

ANNA: What?

ADAM: Eventually! Why does everything always turn into such a fucking drama! You're just like your mother, you know that? You're just like her right now. I want calm. Let's just calm down.

ANNA: "Adam is so distant from me, I can't bear it. Why did I marry a stone?" She wanted a divorce? You wanted a divorce? And then she got cancer and died? *That's* the story of my mother? Do not touch me! Don't you touch me! She says she thinks you cheated on her. Did you?

ADAM: We both screwed around.

ANNA: *(Broken.)* With who?

Beat.

ADAM: *(Very nervous.)* There was this one woman –

ANNA: *(Panic.)* I don't want to hear it.

ADAM: For God sakes, Anna! We weren't saints. Your mother
in particular was an extremely free spirit. I don't know
what period of time that journal covers but ... We did love
each other. And we loved you. And you didn't hear the
fights because we fought in the yard. I did grieve. I don't
know what she wrote about me, but I tried. I really did. It
just ... I was away so much. And at the beginning, when
I came home ... food on the table and pretty dresses ...
Everyone was a homemaker in Texas. I got offered a post
in Japan. I wanted very much to take it. I thought it would
be good for you. See the world. Learn Japanese. What
a wonderful childhood, I thought. Your mother refused.
That was the beginning of a coldness. And something got
broken. No more pretty dresses. Suddenly not a happy
woman, not a happy woman, suddenly. Suddenly she
wants more. More than the house, more than the baby.
And then the eighties, the nineteen eighties ... When I first
served women weren't even allowed in active combat.
Now ... And they're good at it! It's the darndest thing.
Rosie used to tell me "there's not so much difference
between a man and a woman." I laughed in her face.
And now. What do I see? In combat, with a gun, the one
could be the other! And she told me all this. She told me
years ago. I was limited. Anna, I admit it. I limited her.
I see that now. But we were kids! You're in your thirties,
you and Sean are only moving in together now! Please
don't take this so hard.

ANNA: I'm packing my bags and I'm going to the airport and
I'm waiting for a flight home.

ADAM: Don't do that ...

ANNA: I thought the reason you were so cold and distant was
because you were crippled with grief. But I was wrong.
You're just cold and distant. I've put so much energy into
trying to reach you. Being early to our dinners. Dressing
up for you. Always trying to entertain you. No point. She
married a stone.

She exits.

ADAM: Anna!

SCENE TWELVE
A PSYCHIATRIC WARD, NYC

HELENA in an enormous hospital gown. SEAN visiting her.

SEAN: How are you?

HELENA: That's a joke, right.

SEAN: Right. *(Beat.)* I brought you some books and some magazines and stuff.

HELENA: Thanks.

SEAN: Although I see they're not short on board games here. *(Beat.)* And this is chicken soup and some chicken sandwiches. I thought the food here would probably be pretty awful.

HELENA: You made these?

SEAN: Yes. I cook.

HELENA: I forgot. Anna said. You're really good at it.

SEAN: Anna doesn't eat enough. Always picking at things. Works too much. *(Beat.)* She wanted to be here. I was the one who told her to wait until I'd checked on you. Her plane had only just landed there when she got your message.

HELENA: Where's she gone this time?

SEAN: Some conference in France. She's giving a paper.

HELENA: She travels all the time now.

SEAN: Yup. I've barely seen her since we moved in together.

HELENA: She's busy, busy, busy. I had to talk to a psychiatrist this morning so that he could medicate me. I'm currently medicated, I don't know if you can tell. And he said I simply have too much time on my hands. As simple as that. Simple, simple, simple. I said to him "are you saying that if I worked in a bank none of this would be happening" and do you know what he said? "I'd put money on it." And I said "then you'd lose your money, doc, because if I worked in a bank then I *would* kill myself."

SEAN: They are going to let you out again, right?

HELENA: Exactly. I checked myself into rehab but I can't check myself out. I have to be released into somebody's care. My Mom is driving up from Arlington. Tomorrow.

SEAN: Don't you hate your mom?

HELENA: Yes.

SEAN: That doesn't sound like a good plan.

HELENA: I don't have a fucking plan. I have to be released into someone's care.

SEAN: What about me and Anna?

HELENA: What about you?

SEAN: There's our care.

HELENA: It's too much.

SEAN: It's fine.

HELENA: No. It's too much. I should go home. My parents have money. They can pay to get me some … whatever it is I need …

SEAN: I'm free all day. If you want company.

HELENA: What will we talk about?

SEAN: Did Anna tell you about the journal?

HELENA: Her Mom's journal? Uh huh.

SEAN: She won't talk about it. She's gone silent. Like a ghost.

HELENA: That's how she was when I first met her. Like a ghost. Her mom had just died. She appeared at boarding school. A mystery. Never said a word to anyone.

SEAN: How did you get her to open up? She said you guys used to talk to each other after lights were out, that she'd cry in your arms.

HELENA: I asked her lots of questions, I guess. I don't really remember. We were both always the last people picked for softball. It was a common bond.

SEAN: I ask her questions. She says she doesn't want to talk about it.

HELENA: Push her. You have to push her.

SEAN sighs.

SEAN: Sorry. You don't want to hear about our problems.

HELENA: I do. It's comforting. What's the worst thing? What's the worse thing about where you guys are at right now?

SEAN: The not knowing. Not knowing if we're going to end up together. We've been together so long and we're totally lost.

HELENA: That sounds awful.

SEAN: It's like floating on a sea, scanning the horizon for land and you know it's out there but … No plan. It feels like we're drifting. In the land of not-knowing.

HELENA: That's where I live.

SEAN: Hi.

HELENA: Hi.

SCENE THIRTEEN
A HOSPITAL BED, DC

KAY is propped up but her eyes are closed. Somewhere a machine beeps. ADAM watches her. Silence for a while, then ...

KAY: Just, Christ, say something. Don't just sit there and watch me die.

ADAM: I thought you fell asleep.

KAY: No I didn't, although with your conversation I might as well have.

ADAM: I'm sorry.

KAY: Talk. Tell me something classified. Come on. My lips are sealed. I'll take it to the grave.

ADAM: The government was responsible for 9/11.

KAY: Really?

ADAM: No.

KAY: *(Amused.)* You're such an asshole.

Pause.

ADAM: Are you in pain?

KAY: There's no pain. They've got me on all sorts of wonderful things. The only problem is I'll be asleep any second. I drop off, just like that.

ADAM: That's OK. I'm here for a while. I took a few weeks off.

KAY: Why did you do that?

ADAM: Why do you think?

KAY: I haven't got a few weeks.

ADAM: Who knows with you? You're a miracle.

KAY: Not any more.

ADAM: Always.

KAY: I don't want you here. Getting mushy.

ADAM: I won't –

KAY: I'm going out of this world the way I came in. All by
myself. That's the way I want it. And don't you feel sad, or
bad, or anything. I'm off to see the end of the world.

ADAM tries to control his emotions.

KAY: How's Anna? Give me a final installment.

ADAM: Barely talking to me. I told her I was coming East but
… it's probably just a coincidence but she had to go to a
conference. Toronto. She's been giving a lot of papers this
year. Doing incredibly well.

KAY: At least you skipped New York. That must have made
you happy.

ADAM: No, no. I flew in to New York anyway. Saw Sean.
Gave him another karate lesson. He's a good man, a
very good man. He's clearly devoted to her. Rosie would
have approved, he's very much a new man. He does
nearly all of the cooking, he told me. Loves to cook.

KAY: He sounds like quite a guy.

ADAM: He is. I really think he is.

KAY: I'm glad. I always wanted everything to work out great
for her. It had to be so tough losing her mother like that.
(Beat.) I don't even know what she looks like.

ADAM: Would you like to meet her?

KAY: What real, live, in person?

ADAM: Yes.

KAY: I thought she wasn't talking to you.

ADAM: I could try.

KAY: I don't need to meet her. I like thinking of her knocking them dead in Toronto with a man in her kitchen waiting for her to come home.

ADAM: But I'd like you to meet her.

KAY: Too late.

ADAM: Do you want to see a photograph?

He gets a book out of his bag – ANNA's book. ANNA's picture is on the dust jacket.

KAY: That her? This her book?

ADAM: Yes.

KAY: Boy. Weighs a ton.

ADAM: I know.

KAY: You can tell her some time that when she died her hair blue I was the one who told you to get over it. *(Beat.)* Now get her book off my chest before it stops my heart completely.

ADAM takes the book.

ADAM: Can I hold your hand?

KAY: What do you think?

Long pause. He takes her hand.

SCENE FOURTEEN
ANNA AND HELENA ON THE TELEPHONE

HELENA is calling. She's in North Carolina.

ANNA: *(To HELENA.)* Hey!

HELENA: Hey! I didn't think you were going to pick up.

ANNA: I just got in. How is it?

HELENA: I've moved to a town that only has seven hundred and forty people in it, how do you think it is? *(No response.)* I feel so weird being back in the *South*, because as you know I have a lot of *shame* about it ...

ANNA: Yeah, I just walked through the door. I heard your message. Your message said "help."

HELENA: You know what? I was trying to be funny. But I guess that's not so funny.

ANNA: It frightened me.

HELENA: Oh honey, I'm sorry. It's OK. I'm OK here. I love it. I can tell I'll love it. You know what? It is so beautiful. The trees around here, and the mountains – they are just gorgeous. And there are *stars*. You can see stars out here, Anna. I'm going over to my front door right now and ... I'm looking at stars.

She opens her front door. Sure enough, stars. She sits down on her doorstep looking up.

ANNA: When does school start?

HELENA: Tomorrow. A lecture. "Fundamentals of Massage: The Science of Touch."

ANNA: The *Science* of Touch. I like it.

HELENA: How are you?

ANNA: Working like crazy.

HELENA: How's Sean?

ANNA: Fine.

HELENA: Just fine?

ANNA: Yeah.

HELENA: So you guys are great?

ANNA: I'm worried I want to break up with him.

HELENA: Huh …

ANNA: I catch myself imagining he's having sex with someone else and I burst in and then I'm allowed. I'm allowed to leave him. The other day I was teaching and I suddenly imagined he had cancer, he was dying, and I was happy! Because then I could meet somebody else. I feel like I'm going to throw up?

HELENA: Are you OK? Anna?

ANNA: It's just … my heart's pounding.

HELENA: Are you sitting down?

ANNA: No.

HELENA: Sit down. And breathe. *(Beat .)*Are you sitting down? Are you breathing?

ANNA: I actually feel like I'm going to have a panic attack …

HELENA: Honey? Are you sitting?

ANNA: Yes! I'm sitting. Sorry.

HELENA: That's OK.

Silence. ANNA breathes.

ANNA: I am freaking out. I am freaking out. What if I want to break up with him?

HELENA: Can you talk? Do you think you can talk about it without having a panic attack? Or should we just stick with breathing? Because I can sit here on the other end of the phone with you and just breathe. I have got no problem with that. I have got all night.

ANNA: Everything's fine, between us, nothing's happened, it's just … I can't bear for him to touch me. Not at the moment. I sleep pushed up against the wall.

HELENA: You don't need to make a decision about anything right now. When your body's ready to make a decision it will make a decision. It will stay or go. You don't need to over think it.

ANNA: OK. I don't want to talk about it any more, OK?

HELENA: No problemo. How's the new book coming? Emily Dickenson?

ANNA: No time to write it. People keep asking me for articles about Keats. He's become my life partner. Could I be any more fucking esoteric and obscure?

HELENA: It's not just about Keats. It's not just about grammar. It's about art. It's about indicating, right, indicating, what is it you say in your book? That "seemingly insignificant details result in beauty!" I mean, that's what you're devoting your life to! To beauty! And if we don't have beauty then what's the point of progressing! What's the point of recovering from cancer? What's the point of anything?

ANNA: God, I love you.

SCENE FIFTEEN
A THRESHOLD, IRELAND

ANNA and LINDA sit with their backsides squarely inside the house and their legs outside. Bright sunlight. LINDA might wear sunglasses.

LINDA: The weather's not always like this, you know. This is very unusual weather for Ireland.

ANNA: That's what Sean said.

LINDA: You've been very lucky weather-wise.

ANNA: Yup.

LINDA: I must say it's been a pleasure meeting you. You're very nice.

ANNA: Thank you.

LINDA: No really. You're very, very, nice. I hope you'll come again.

ANNA: I hope so too.

LINDA: We've been like ships in the night, haven't we? All
Seany's fault. You're a pleasure, you've been a pleasure.
I was really nervous before you came, you know? I was
incredibly nervous. The night before you arrived, I was
up all night worrying about how to pretend to be a totally
different person for a week but then you came and I hadn't
the energy and then we had a little drink and we got on
fine, didn't we?

ANNA: Absolutely.

LINDA: I shall miss you.

ANNA: It's not over. There's still two more days.

LINDA: Sean will be back with the sandwiches soon. Won't he
be surprised? Seeing me on the front step.

ANNA: How are you feeling?

LINDA: Fine. I feel fine. That Xanax really is something.

ANNA: I'll leave you a few.

LINDA: I would never have thought that a tiny little pill could
have such a huge effect. I mean, I'm not one hundred
percent, you know. I wouldn't say that. I know that I'm
frightened in my head. But my heart … steady as a rock.
Incredible.

ANNA: I use them for flying.

LINDA: How do you get them?

ANNA: My friend Helena gave them to me.

LINDA: Is that legal?

ANNA: Absolutely not.

LINDA: Did your friend Helena not want to keep them for
herself?

ANNA: No. Her mother, who is a psychiatrist, mails them to her. But Helena won't take them because she thinks it's her mother's way of trying to control her.

LINDA: Interesting people you know out there. *(Beat.)* I honestly can't believe I'm sitting on the step. If a neighbor walks by they'll shit.

ANNA: Is it people you're frightened of, or space?

LINDA: Oh I don't know. It's that there's a world out there. *(Beat.)* The attack was so long ago, I wonder if maybe even that has nothing to do with it. Maybe I was always to end up this way. Born with a deficiency of something.

ANNA: You haven't ended up this way. It's where you are right now.

LINDA: My brother says it would have been easier on me if they'd caught him. But they never did. I was no help at all. He was all a haze to me, you see. It was a day like this, a rare day, a warm day, and I fell asleep, and by the time I woke up again the mist was coming in, the light was leaving, and ... I couldn't give the police a single detail. They said it was shock. They said he shocked all the details out of my head. My pretty little head. I overheard the doctor and that's what he said. He said "the bastard shocked every detail out of her pretty little head."

ANNA: I can't imagine ...

LINDA: So no he was never caught.

ANNA: Most, I believe, aren't.

LINDA: That's right. Running free. When I can't sleep I imagine they found the one who did it. I get a telephone call. "Hello Linda," they say. "We've found him." So I go down to the station. They take me to a black room. A cell. He's chained up. Handcuffed. And they leave me alone with my man in the mist. And I walk up to his chair and I ... Oh Lord. If you knew ... you'd be amazed with the kind of things my imagination comes up with. Still. A long time ago. No need to be maudlin.

Pause.

ANNA: After lunch, Sean wants to take a walk along the cliffs. He says there's no view more beautiful.

LINDA: It was always his favorite place.

ANNA: So he's says.

LINDA: *(Meaningfully.)* I know he really wants to take you there. *(Beat.)* There's heather, purple for miles just about. And you walk and you walk and there's only sea ahead of you. You're standing on an edge of the world. *(Beat.)* Shall we go in, have a nice cup of tea?

ANNA: I thought you wanted Sean to see you on the step. *(Beat.)* You'll make his day. *(Beat.)* I bet Claire would do this with you, if you wanted her too. Once in a while.

LINDA: Don't get your hopes up. You're not The Miracle Worker.

ANNA: Listen, I'm an American. I am terminally optimistic. I want to you to visit us in the States.

LINDA: *(Scoffing, but pleased.)* Visit you in the States. Have we not established that I'm batshit crazy?

ANNA: Maybe one day you'll find yourself on a plane to America. See where we live. You've only seen a photograph of our apartment. And our apartment has only seen a photograph of you.

LINDA: A photograph?

ANNA: Sure. You're on the bookcase.

LINDA: What am I doing there?

ANNA: You're framed.

Pause.

LINDA: Fresh life. That's what you are.

SCENE SIXTEEN
THE WOODS OF NORTH CAROLINA

HELENA marches, intrepid, through the woods. Finding a clearing, she stops and prepares herself and the space for meditation. Ready, she crosses her legs, closes her eyes and begins.

Enough silence to hear. Then a growl. The growl comes from a BEAR. HELENA opens one eye. She sees nothing troubling. She resumes her meditation.

Behind her, GIDEON enters. He has a rifle pointed beyond HELENA, off stage. HELENA hears GIDEON's footsteps, opens her eyes again, sees the gun. HELENA offers up an earsplitting scream. Confusion.

GIDEON: Shhhh!

HELENA: What the fuck do you want? What the fuck do you want from me?

GIDEON: Ma'am … ma'am …

HELENA: I knew it! I knew it that one day I'd be raped!

GIDEON: Get down on the ground. I need you to stay very quiet.

HELENA: I bet you do you filthy son of a bitch!

GIDEON: There is a bear behind you.

HELENA whirls around and sees the bear. She screams again, even more loudly if possible and then throws herself to the ground and curls up into a tiny little ball.

HELENA: Oh my God, oh my God, oh my God …

GIDEON: Stay calm now …

HELENA: Is this because I have my period?

GIDEON: This is because we're walking about where bears live.

HELENA: Is he still there?

GIDEON: It's a lady bear and yes she is. She's just watching us.

HELENA: Are you going to kill her?

GIDEON: Only if she charges.

HELENA: So we just wait?

GIDEON: That's right. That's what we do for the minute.

Beat.

HELENA: Now what's happening?

GIDEON: Not much. She's just looking right at you.

HELENA: At me?

GIDEON: That's what she's doing right now.

HELENA: Can I look at her?

GIDEON: Sure. Sure you can. Just don't make direct eye contact.

From her fetal position, HELENA sneaks a peek at the bear.

GIDEON: You know what we're going to do? We're going to back away slowly …

HELENA gets up, cautiously, staring at the bear.

HELENA: I am making eye contact …

GIDEON: Ma'am, she's going to perceive that as a challenge –

HELENA: She's looking at me, I'm looking at her. "for I am as ugly as a bear, for beasts that meet me run away for fear." But she's not ugly. And she's not running away.

HELENA is crying. But for the first time in her life she cries tears of joy.

HELENA: You're not ugly …

HELENA starts walking towards the bear.

GIDEON: Lady –

HELENA: We're not ugly …

GIDEON: Woman, get away from that bear, she'll rip your fucking head off.

HELENA: I don't think so ….

GIDEON shoots, HELENA charges him.

HELENA: No!

She knocks GIDEON to the ground, landing on top of him. This is not an un-erotic moment for either of them.

GIDEON: There now. She's taking off.

HELENA: Are you blind? We were communing. I was communing with her and you betrayed the *trust* –

GIDEON: No …

HELENA: Yes.

GIDEON: I just saved your life, you crazy bitch.

HELENA: My. What happened to ma'am?

GIDEON: I just saved your life, Ma'am.

HELENA: Helena.

GIDEON: Helena. Gideon.

HELENA: Nice to meet you, I suppose.

GIDEON: You were not having a moment with that bear.

HELENA: No, I was. It was quite a profound moment actually. Until you spoiled it with your gun.

GIDEON: *(Grinning.)* Are you on 'shrums? Can I have some?

HELENA: You can make fun all you want but I looked in her eyes and she looked into my eyes and it was … it was life-changing actually. I saw total acceptance. And she was feeling some –

GIDEON: Bears feel only three things. Hungry. Sleepy. And like they need to take a shit. They're a lot like men in that way.

HELENA: Oh God.

GIDEON: What?

HELENA: I hate it when men limit themselves like that. You can be so much more. You can be sensitive, and loving and complex and broken and …

GIDEON: *(Slowly.)* I find you *fascinating* …

HELENA: You do?

GIDEON: Where you from?

HELENA: I was living in New York but I moved out here just a few weeks ago.

GIDEON: That's a change of pace.

HELENA: Yup.

GIDEON: Well I've been out here fifteen years and they still call me a newcomer.

HELENA: What does that make me?

GIDEON: A baby.

HELENA: Where'd you move from?

GIDEON: Mississippi.

HELENA: I was also raised in the South.

GIDEON: No kidding, you're a Southern girl?

HELENA: Arlington , VA …

GIDEON: Well Helena, the South welcomes you back home. Welcome home.

HELENA kisses him on the lips.

GIDEON: Me and my wife should have you over for dinner some night.

Pause.

HELENA: Wow, you're married. That is great, that is so great. When did you get married?

GIDEON: Going on twelve years now.

HELENA: High school sweethearts?

GIDEON: Met in a bar.

HELENA: Any kids?

GIDEON: Six.

Beat.

HELENA: Six? You have six kids?

GIDEON: Ben, Megan, Rachel, Christian, Nick, and little Bethy.

HELENA: There's really no common ground here. Wow. Can I ask you something?

GIDEON: Shoot.

HELENA: How old are you?

GIDEON: I'm thirty-four.

HELENA: I'm thirty four.

GIDEON: Something in common, then.

SCENE SEVENTEEN
LINDA'S HOUSE, IRELAND

Lunchtime.

LINDA: Anna is just lovely.

ADAM: Oh, I like Sean very much. Great guy.

LINDA: Good kids.

ADAM: Yes they are.

LINDA: I need to talk to you about the wedding. Before they get back. To get to those cliffs you have to walk.

ADAM: Anna said it's quite a way.

LINDA: Twenty minutes across the heather.

ADAM: Anna said you're a little agoraphobic.

LINDA: That's right.

ADAM: I was surprised when they told me where they were getting married. Seems a little selfish of them.

LINDA: No, they asked me. When they came back to tell me they were getting married, Sean said "Mammy we'd like to do it on the cliffs." And what could I say? I said "I think that's perfect."

ADAM: Are you concerned you won't be able to ... should we push for a change of venue, do you think? After all the weather is against us anyway.

LINDA: No. I will walk on my two legs to those cliffs and I will stand there and watch my son marry. I promise you that. I wanted to tell you I was afraid. I might need your arm. I might need a man on steady legs beside me, understanding. My brother will be there but so will his wife. He'll be taken up with her, she'll probably be complaining about getting her heels stuck in the mud or something.

ADAM: I'd be happy to.

LINDA: Maybe take my arm or something.

ADAM: No problem.

LINDA: Thank you. Sean said you've traveled all over the world, seen all kinds of things, fought all kinds of battles you're not even allowed to talk about. He looks up to you. *(Beat.)* I expect you're almost never afraid.

ADAM: I was afraid ten minutes ago. I was afraid to ring your doorbell. A strange country, a strange house.

LINDA: It's kind of you to tell me that.

ADAM: I was afraid to get on the airplane. Afraid to come. All by myself. No wife. No … no other person. I will be grateful for your arm on the day of the wedding.

LINDA: I used to go to the cliffs all the time when I was a girl. Sean's right. It is the most beautiful view in all the world. *(Beat.)* I was raped there when Sean was eight years old. That was the last time I went.

ADAM: Do the kids understand what they're asking you to do?

LINDA: Not at all. They know that it happened. They don't know where. I would never tell them. This man, he took away many things from me, he never knew, I think, he was taking. There was a child. I aborted the child. The church aborted me. My husband left. My son and daughter grew up with a useless mother and no father at all. But I would not let this man destroy Sean's favorite place in all the world. And now I'm going back to watch my son marry there. And perhaps now *I* win.

SCENE EIGHTEEN
LINDA'S HOUSE, DONEGAL

LINDA, ADAM, MAX, HELENA all talking loudly, on top of each other, as big families do. That's the important thing. A cacophony.

MAX: It's going to rain –

HELENA: But Anna says –

LINDA: Sean is dead set on –

MAX: The forecast says rain, my darlings.

LINDA: What does it matter if people get wet? It's a tiny wedding.

HELENA: These are friends! They won't care if –

ADAM: But you have to consider, people have flown in.

HELENA: Is there a way we can erect a tent?

MAX: Not by tomorrow morning.

LINDA: The weather forecast isn't always right, you know.
In fact it's always wrong!

Black out. The sound of bells, not wedding bells, but a clock striking the time. Then, a howling wind.

SCENE NINETEEN
THE CLIFFS OF DONEGAL

We see the people we know – ADAM, LINDA, and MAX, standing in raincoats. The rest of the CAST is on stage, as WEDDING GUESTS.

HELENA fights to make herself heard above the wind.

HELENA: Hello, I'm Helena and I will be officiating today.
This is the first time I have done this so as you can imagine I am both excited and a little nervous – much as I imagine Anna and Sean are. It is after all the first time that they have done this too. I am not here as a representative of any church, or of any state. I have not been arbitrarily ordained on the internet. I am here not to marry them but to witness with all of you as they choose to marry each other. And what we are witnessing is the birth of a new family.

The wedding scene remains, at least at first, but what we hear, and probaby see, is ANNA and SEAN late at night, their first real conversation.

SEAN: Tell me about where you grew up. The place you were born.

ANNA: Countryside.

SEAN: Yeah?

ANNA: Tall grass. Watercolor colors. That kind of thing. A lot of space. A lot of sunshine. A lot of play. I was a happy child. I didn't see my father much –

SEAN: How come?

ANNA: He's in the military.

SEAN: Army?

ANNA nods.

ANNA: When I did it was a treat, and when he was gone I had my mother all to myself. That's what every child wants anyway. I was lucky. Very, very lucky I think. Of course that's what made it so hard when she died. That she was my best friend. My therapist says –

SEAN: You have a therapist?

ANNA: Uh huh. *(Pause.)* This is New York City, that's what we do.

SEAN: Sure.

ANNA: Wow.

SEAN: What?

ANNA: You're making me feel really uncomfortable.

SEAN: Why?

ANNA: Because I say I have a therapist and a fucking cloud covers your face like

SEAN: No.

ANNA: Yes.

SEAN: I've dated a lot of crazies.

ANNA: Were they in therapy?

SEAN: No.

ANNA: There you go.

Pause.

SEAN: I'm sorry. I interrupted. What does your therapist say? About your mother?

ANNA: Never mind.

SEAN: I'm sorry.

ANNA: She said that my mother died before I had a chance to rebel against her. So it made her death particularly …

SEAN: Sure. *(Beat.)* My father died of a heart attack when I was eighteen.

ANNA: I'm sorry.

SEAN: I hadn't seen him for years. He left my mother. I think I stopped loving him. When he died I felt sad. But relieved almost. Free.

ANNA: I don't like the word "crazies." I like the word "troubled." You've dated a lot of *troubled* women.

SEAN: Have I?

ANNA: Apparently. *(Beat.)* I'm not troubled any more. Fragile sometimes, but I'm not troubled.

SEAN: That's nice.

ANNA: Tell me about where *you* grew up.

SEAN: Town. Covered in mist usually. Small town. Stony. Grey. Near the sea.

ANNA: Happy?

SEAN: No. Not me. I wasn't. Sometimes I was. But mostly sad. My mother was very sad you see. Something bad happened to her and she never got over it. So when I was growing up the sadness was like the mist, you know. Fucking everywhere.

ANNA: It's awful, isn't it?

SEAN: What is?

ANNA: Getting to know someone.

SCENE TWENTY
TWO FIGURES, BRIEFLY ILLUMINATED

ANNA and SEAN are the only people on stage. They are somewhere quiet.

SEAN: A few drops of rain never hurt anybody.

ANNA: Could you even hear what you were agreeing to?

SEAN: I could hear. Could you?

ANNA: Yes.

SEAN: It was perfect.

ANNA: It was perfect.

>*Pause.*

SEAN: I wish we didn't have to die.

ANNA: We won't. Not for a long time yet. Not for a long time.

>*End of play.*

PARENTS' EVENING

Parents' Evening was first produced by the Cherry Lane Theatre in New York as part of their Mentor Project on May 7, 2003. The performance was directed by Irina Brown, with costumes by Yvonne DeMoravia, lights by Brian Aldous, sound by Bart Fasbender, and props by Faye Armon. The Production Stage Manager was Kate Hefel. The cast was as follows:

MOTHER	Lisa Emery
FATHER	Ken Marks

Parents' Evening was later produced by the Flea Theater in New York on April 17, 2010. The performance was directed by Jim Simpson, with sets by Jerad Schomer, costumes by Claudia Brown, and lights by Brian Aldous. The Production Stage Manager was Carrie-Dell Furay. The cast was as follows:

MOTHER	Julianne Nicholson
FATHER	James Waterston

Characters

Mother (30s/40s)

Father (30s/40s)

Time and Place
Late 20th Century, a city.

Act One

The only thing that there needs to be on stage is a double bed. Anything else can be actual or suggested and should fade into the darkness of the rest of the stage, so that what we see is a small glimpse of a world floating in the island of the theatre.

The MOTHER has just come in the room. She is looking at some papers.

It is early evening.

FATHER: You were in with her for a long time.

MOTHER: She was upset.

FATHER: She was supposed to be upset. If she can't win gracefully then she shouldn't play.

MOTHER: She got excited.

FATHER: Oh so excited. Making up a little victory song. And then just singing it over and over again. 'I've won, you're dumb.' I mean that doesn't even rhyme.

MOTHER: It's a half rhyme.

FATHER: She took no pleasure in our company. Just wanted to roll over us like a fucking tank and win as quickly as possible.

MOTHER: The object of the game is to win, Michael.

FATHER: The object is to provide pleasant social interaction. That's what a game's for. That's why they were invented. They are meant to be a communal experience. Not an opportunity for our daughter to plot our destruction and then actually snort with glee once she's achieved it.

MOTHER: We ought to start her on Scrabble. It would be good for her vocabulary. And her spelling.

Beat.

FATHER: I'll tell you what I don't understand about Clue. Why would you kill someone with a candlestick, if there was a revolver available?

Beat.

I don't know. Gloating. It was disgusting. That is a bad habit.

MOTHER: I explained to her that it wasn't nice.

FATHER: For an hour?

MOTHER: No. And then we just talked.

FATHER: And what were you talking about?

MOTHER: She told me about her day.

FATHER: And how was her day?

MOTHER: She trespassed. On someone's property. During her lunch break.

FATHER: She what?

MOTHER: She went trespassing. I scolded her.

FATHER: Whose property?

MOTHER: I have no idea.

FATHER: She can't do that.

MOTHER: I know. That's what I told her.

FATHER: Jesus.

MOTHER: It's alright. She's consumed with guilt.

FATHER: That's all a big performance.

MOTHER: It wasn't a performance. By the time she told me she'd got herself so upset she could hardly breathe. But I calmed her down. We talked about it.

FATHER: I'm sure that's why she does these things. She does evil all day then pays penance in the evening and she knows perfectly well you'll absolve her. What did you do? Tell her to say a couple of Hail Mary's?

MOTHER: I told her not to do it again.

FATHER: That's it?

MOTHER: And I got her to talk about why she'd done it ...

FATHER: And?

MOTHER: The other kids went.

FATHER: I don't like those kids she's hanging around with. That girl Victoria is a thug.

MOTHER: Her mother's a potter.

FATHER: Well her daughter's a criminal. Trespassing. Thank God they weren't caught. Were they?

MOTHER: Not as far as I know.

FATHER: I suppose the police would have contacted us by now.

MOTHER: I'll tell you who else wants to contact us.

FATHER: Who?

MOTHER: Sarah Barnes' mother.

FATHER: Oh God, what's Jessica done?

MOTHER: I don't know. Nothing. When Anne-Marie picked Jessica up from school today Mrs. Barnes told her to tell us that Jessica lent Sarah a book that apparently is inappropriate.

FATHER: Inappropriate how?

MOTHER: It was about sex.

FATHER: What does the woman want us to do? Censor Jessica's reading?

MOTHER: I know. I think it's fine, really. Jessica told me about it. It's teenage fiction. Young couple, they fall in love, they have sex.

FATHER: Well Jessica knows about sex.

MOTHER: And then they have oral sex.

Beat.

FATHER: Well she's read it now.

MOTHER: Yes, but it's one of a series.

FATHER: Oh.

MOTHER: She wants to read the rest of them.

FATHER: I see.

MOTHER: There are nine.

FATHER: Nine? What do they do by the end?

MOTHER: I have no idea.

FATHER: I wonder if we've done it …

MOTHER: The kids are hooked.

FATHER: I bet they are.

MOTHER: Mrs Barnes was upset. She wants to speak to us about it this evening.

FATHER: At least the kids are exchanging books. That's positive.

MOTHER: Not according to Mrs. Barnes. We'll have to spend the whole time avoiding her.

FATHER: I think we should tell her to fuck off. She can censor her own child's reading. I'm not censoring mine. And where does she get off communicating with us through the babysitter?

MOTHER: Do you really think we should let Jessica read them all?

FATHER: Yes. Who wrote them?

MOTHER: I don't know.

FATHER: They sound like crap.

MOTHER: They're not crap. They're educational. Now angel, I just have to finish this before we go.

The MOTHER goes back to her papers.

FATHER: Maybe I should see if Jessica wants to sign a peace treaty.

MOTHER: She's engrossed in book number three.

FATHER: Maybe we should buy her some D. H. Lawrence.

MOTHER: It's too hard.

FATHER: Look, I don't mind Jessica reading books with sexual content, but she should read good ones. Let's get her some D.H Lawrence.

MOTHER: It's too hard for her, Michael. She's ten!

FATHER: We could read it to her. Then if she has any questions …

MOTHER: I am not reading Jessica D. H. Lawrence.

FATHER: At least Lawrence is good.

MOTHER: He isn't very good, and he's extremely explicit.

The MOTHER goes back to her work.

FATHER: I think he's good. *(No response.)* Is there anything else I should know? So far we've covered her gloating, her increasing criminality and her filthy books.

The MOTHER looks up.

MOTHER: We talked about tonight.

FATHER: Is she nervous?

MOTHER: Slightly. She explained in great detail that Miss Broderick hates her, but it's not her fault.

FATHER: Which one's Miss Broderick?

MOTHER: The music teacher. Oh and Jessica gave me a form from her. She has to choose an instrument to play at school for next year.

FATHER: Really? That's nice. Is that something we're supposed to discuss with them this evening?

MOTHER: No. It's up to Jessica.

FATHER: What does she want to play?

MOTHER: Well she says trumpet.

FATHER: Oh fucking typical.

MOTHER: It's not terribly feminine. Not that it necessarily matters.

FATHER: Why can't she play the harp? Or what about the flute? Or the piano. What about the piano?

MOTHER: She wants to play the trumpet.

FATHER: It's all very well wanting to play the trumpet when you're ten. When you're thirty who cares? Unless you're actually a professional trumpeter.

MOTHER: It's what she wants.

FATHER: I think we should talk about this.

He waits until the MOTHER looks up from her papers.

It's a very important decision, Judy. What instrument she plays. I think she should play the piano or something.

MOTHER: Then talk to her about it.

FATHER: Do you think she should play the piano?

MOTHER: I don't really care, Michael. I think she should play whatever she wants.

FATHER: What about the violin?

MOTHER: No way. I refuse to listen to her scratching out tunes on a violin for the next five years. It would be unbearable. Not that the trumpet's going to be much better.

FATHER: When do we have to hand in the form?

Pause.

MOTHER: I don't know. Next week?

FATHER: I'll talk to her about the piano.

FATHER: I think she's quite musical.

MOTHER: As she demonstrated tonight with her little song.

FATHER: The song was unpleasant. But the impulse was creative. That's good. Maybe she'll become a great artist.

MOTHER: Well I tell you, she can't paint. A client came in the other day, noticed one of Jessica's pictures in my office, and assumed she was five. I didn't say anything.

FATHER: Five?

MOTHER: Five.

FATHER: Look, I know she can't paint. You're the one who's always telling her she can.

MOTHER: I'm being encouraging.

FATHER: It just makes her arrogant. She holds up a piece of paper she's been splashing paint on for two minutes, says 'it's good isn't it,' and you say 'yes.' I think we need to convey to her that a piece of art doesn't take two minutes.

MOTHER: It's alright, darling. You've made it very clear that it takes at least ten years.

FATHER: You know I do write all day. I don't just sit here and do nothing. And I don't bring it straight to you and say 'it's good, isn't it.' I mean, really …

MOTHER: What am I supposed to say to her? That it's bad?

FATHER: I did.

MOTHER: When?

FATHER: The other day. She said 'it's good isn't it,' I said 'no,' she said 'why,' I said 'because it's taken you two minutes.' She tried again. It was slightly better. I said so.

Beat.

MOTHER: Did you say it was "slightly better" or "better?"

FATHER: Better. I said it was better.

The MOTHER returns to her papers.

I told her I liked that poem though, didn't I? I thought that was wonderful. Really wonderful.

MOTHER: I know you did.

FATHER: Didn't you?

MOTHER: No, I thought it was awful.

FATHER: What?

MOTHER: What? It was.

FATHER: Judy, it was brilliant.

MOTHER: It didn't make sense.

FATHER: It did make sense. 'All's quiet, everyone's working. The only sound is of pencils writing.' There's real rhythm to that.

MOTHER: How can all be quiet if the only sound is of pencils writing?

FATHER: Because 'quiet' doesn't necessarily mean no sound. *(Whispering.)* This is quiet.

Beat.

I thought it was exceptional. I xeroxed it.

Beat.

Will you read it again?

MOTHER: Yes.

FATHER: But will you? I've stuck it to my filing cabinet.

MOTHER: Yes Michael. But right now I have to finish this.

The MOTHER works. The FATHER looks into his closet to select his clothes for the evening.

FATHER: Why you want me dressed up for this I have no idea. It just makes me more tense.

The FATHER stares into his closet.

What would you like me to wear?

MOTHER: A suit.

FATHER: Right. This is absolutely ridiculous.

MOTHER: I don't want to go either, Michael.

FATHER: I hate schools. They're such fascist institutions. They always make you feel like you're going to get into trouble.

MOTHER: Last year you did get into trouble. You made the history teacher cry.

FATHER: Because that wall display was bullshit!

MOTHER: It wasn't bullshit.

FATHER: Judy it was total bullshit. The "olden days." When were they? What time period exactly is the time period of horses and carriages and lots of vegetables in baskets?

MOTHER: Michael it was designed for people less than a decade old.

FATHER: No dates. Not a single date. It's a history display! We've got a ten year old in the house who thinks the past is just something that happened in black and white with wagons.

MOTHER: It's a gradual process. Next year they do the Civil War.

FATHER: And that will just be lots of pictures of soldiers and cannons and some poems by Whitman which no one will mention are homoerotic. Let's just see, let's just see, if she knows the dates of the war by the end of the year. I bet she doesn't. I bet the history teacher doesn't know them. I'm extremely tempted to quiz the stupid woman tonight. You remember when I asked her the date of the Boston Tea Party? No idea!

MOTHER: Michael, don't make a scene again.

FATHER: I wasn't going to make a scene. I was just suggesting a little quiz.

MOTHER: Well don't. Don't do anything.

FATHER: We are supposed to be discussing our daughter's education. That's why we're going.

MOTHER: I know but I don't want to be in there for a long time.

FATHER: Judy, this is important.

MOTHER: You know I find these evenings really nerve-wracking. It's bad enough waiting to see how many people are going to tell us that Jessica's a bad influence without worrying that you're going to attack the teachers. Alright?

FATHER: Come on. Everyone knows how bright Jessica is.

MOTHER: It's never about being bright. It's about behavior.

FATHER: Exactly. And that is what's wrong with the way they teach. If Jessica was actually busy learning things she's perfectly capable of, like dates, instead of doing quite so much coloring in, then there wouldn't be time for behavior. Of course she's disruptive. She's bored.

MOTHER: Well let's pray she's been less bored this year because I don't think I can bear another parade of teachers telling us that Jessica's not the only child in the class. God it was embarrassing.

FATHER: I thought they embarrassed themselves.

MOTHER: Perhaps I would have been less embarrassed if I hadn't been fairly sure that while you were making the history teacher cry, the entire room was watching, thinking 'no wonder Jessica's a bad influence, her parents are crazy.'

FATHER: You think they blame us?

MOTHER: Of course they blame us.

FATHER: *(A joke.)* Do they accept no responsibility for her delinquency? *(The MOTHER doesn't react.)* And we're not crazy.

MOTHER: It doesn't matter what we think, does it? It matters what they think.

FATHER: Come on … Don't get worked up. I think together we can handle a gaggle of grade school teachers. Especially all dressed up.

MOTHER: I'm not getting worked up, Michael. I want to finish this.

Beat.

It will take fifteen minutes. Then I'll get ready and we'll go. Alright? All I need now is my green file.

She starts looking through her papers. She looks up, body tensed.

I can't find it. Shit. It's green.

FATHER: Green file.

MOTHER: It's got everything in it.

FATHER: Have you left it downstairs?

MOTHER: It's not downstairs.

FATHER: Sorry.

MOTHER: Shit.

FATHER: It might be downstairs.

MOTHER: If I've lost it I'm in big trouble.

FATHER: You didn't lose it. You never have.

MOTHER: *(Searching.)* I wonder if I left it at work.

FATHER: Did you take it into the bathroom?

MOTHER: Why would I take it into the bathroom? Michael, you're in the way.

FATHER: Jessica's room? Well if you lost it there it's gone forever.

MOTHER: *(Searching.)* Not now, Michael.

FATHER: Fine. But I am going downstairs to enjoy a glass of wine before we leave and maybe, just maybe while I'm sipping it all my myself, I'll spy your green file, buried somewhere beneath the day's debris. *(No response.)* I think I saw a yellow file in the living room.

MOTHER: It's not a yellow file, Michael. It's green! It's my green file!

FATHER: What's the yellow one?

MOTHER: They're my files, Michael. Alright? Just let me think.

FATHER: Why do you scatter them all over the house? Between you and Jessica …

MOTHER: Yes, I know. We're a terrible disappointment to you.

FATHER: You're not a disappointment to me. I just feel like I'm drowning in everyone else's shit. I mean there are papers all over the house. No wonder you can't find anything.

MOTHER: You are not helping.

FATHER: Well let's clean up around here. I mean those photos of Spain have been piled on the mantelpiece for six months, Judy. You promised we were going to put them in an album. When are we going to do it?

MOTHER: I don't know.

FATHER: It just gets depressing. I feel like I spend the whole day wandering through our home sorting through papers I don't know what to do with because they're not mine, and switching off all the lights that Jessica has somehow managed to leave on in every single room in the one hour she has between getting up and going to school. I actually said to her this afternoon 'when you have your own house and you pay the electricity bill, then you can leave the lights on.'

The MOTHER stops her search.

MOTHER: You said that?

FATHER: It's a waste of money.

MOTHER: That is so stupid. That is such a cliché.

FATHER: And our electricity bill is ridiculous. What do you want me to do?

Pause. The MOTHER carries on searching.

FATHER: What if I showed Jessica the electricity bill? We could combine it with long division. How many times would her allowance go into the electricity bill?

MOTHER: Long division makes her cry.

FATHER: Yes, but she needs to learn how to do it and this could be a fun little exercise.

MOTHER: I can't find it. I'll have to finish this, go into work early, and hope to God I left it on my desk.

FATHER: Right. How early?

MOTHER: Early. And on debris, Michael.

FATHER: Debris. Tell me.

MOTHER: You have to flush condoms down the toilet.

FATHER: I can't. It gets clogged. Why?

MOTHER: Because Jessica saw one in our waste basket last week.

FATHER: She what!

MOTHER: She saw one in our waste basket and it upset her.

FATHER: Oh God.

MOTHER: So don't put them in there. Also, it's not nice.

FATHER: What did she say?

MOTHER: She said what's that?

FATHER: And what did you say?

MOTHER: I said that's Daddy's condom.

FATHER: You said it was mine?

MOTHER: It was yours. What did you want me to say?

FATHER: It was ours.

MOTHER: Fine. Next time.

FATHER: And I'm not going to feel fucking ashamed for making love to you! *(No response.)* And she shouldn't just walk in here without knocking.

MOTHER: She did knock. And I hate it.

FATHER: What?

MOTHER: The knocking. It's not natural.

FATHER: Politeness isn't natural. Neither is polished wood, or penicillin or pencil sharpeners but they all make the world a little more bearable.

MOTHER: Knocking on our door like a stranger.

FATHER: What if I'm getting changed?

MOTHER: Well she's already seen your condom.

FATHER: She's knocking on the door.

MOTHER: I told her that when I'm here she doesn't have to knock.

FATHER: Judy, that's not fair.

MOTHER: I don't think it's right that she knocks.

FATHER: What if we knock on her door too? Then it's a mutual respect situation. We respect her space. She respects ours.

MOTHER: I am not knocking on my child's door.

FATHER: I bet she'd like it. We'd be treating her like an adult.

MOTHER: She's not an adult.

FATHER: She is. She's a little adult.

MOTHER: Little adults are dwarves, Michael. She is a child.

Beat.

FATHER: Shall I bring you up a glass of wine?

The MOTHER shakes her head. She's working. He looks at her. A moment.

I called the painters. They're coming on Monday.

MOTHER: Good.

FATHER: I didn't tell you, I spoke to my publishers. They're extending my deadline.

Beat.

So I've got another six months.

MOTHER: Good.

FATHER: I can do it in six months. I just have to figure out how to get Helena over to Portugal. I mean she's there. I've got thirty pages of her in Portugal, having lunch, and talking about Art as Philosophy. And it's very good, right? We agreed I need to keep that section. She has to be there for the lunch at the villa. But why would she suddenly up and go to Portugal? *(Beat. He gasps.)* What if it's because she knows David? *(Then, deflated.)* No, she can't know David before the lunch. Otherwise I'd have to rewrite that walk they have in the orange grove. Oh I don't know. Maybe I should just cut the whole thing.

MOTHER: Michael, I have to do this! Now! We agreed if I came home early you'd leave me time to do this. And since I got home from work I've had to play a fucking board game, calm you and Jessica down, listen to her catalogue of wrongs, listen to your catalogue of complaints about your house, your wife and your child, and now, twenty minutes before we have to go out, you want me to talk about the fucking novel! I've got to be in court tomorrow. I have to read this.

Beat.

FATHER: Maybe I'll drink some wine and listen to some jazz.

The phone rings. The MOTHER answers.

MOTHER: Hello? Oh, hi … Oh fantastic! That's fantastic.

FATHER: I thought you had to work.

The MOTHER ignores him.

MOTHER: Oh Ken, you're an angel!

He stands looking at her.

MOTHER: Oh thank God. Thank you. Thank you … No, just bring it in tomorrow. It's fine, I'm going out tonight anyway … yes, it's Parents Night at the school. I know, I'm terrified. One of the mothers wants to kill us because Jessica's been handing out dirty books …

She laughs at whatever he's saying on the other end.

They didn't … what did Lisa say? That's ridiculous … Oh is she better?

The FATHER sighs heavily.

MOTHER: What did the doctor say?... Oh that's good ...
We're fine ...

The FATHER sighs again, looking at her.

I – no I ... I'm sorry, Ken, I have to go. Yes. Yes. I will. See
you tomorrow ... Thanks.

She hangs up. Beat.

FATHER: Wine and jazz. Off I go.

MOTHER: You have to let me talk on the phone, Michael.

FATHER: I do let you talk on the phone.

MOTHER: No you don't.

FATHER: Of course I do.

MOTHER: Then what was that?

FATHER: You said you were going to work.

MOTHER: Yes I know, but the phone rang.
And anyway that was work. Ken found my file.

FATHER: Great. Good for Ken.

MOTHER: Michael, I mean it. I really can't bear it when you
do that.

FATHER: Do what?

MOTHER: When you look at me like that while I'm on the
phone. I can't talk to anybody.

FATHER: Oh come on.

MOTHER: People comment on it. They're scared to call me here.

FATHER: What are you talking about? People call you all the time.

MOTHER: They don't, Michael.

FATHER: They –

MOTHER: I'm sorry, but they just don't!

FATHER: Judy …

MOTHER: They don't call me here! They don't!

FATHER: Someone just called!

MOTHER: Everyone at work is always taking about how scary it is calling me here. It's a joke. It's an office joke!

FATHER: Who makes jokes about it?

MOTHER: I'm not telling you who.

FATHER: Just tell me.

MOTHER: No.

FATHER: I don't believe it!

MOTHER: You don't hear yourself. You sound unbelievably irritated every time someone asks for me. You sigh at them!

FATHER: I am irritated. They're interrupting.

MOTHER: Interrupting what?

FATHER: We're talking, the phone rings, you start talking to someone else!

MOTHER: What am I supposed to do?

FATHER: Look, if you and I were in the middle of a conversation, and a passerby just walked up and joined in, that wouldn't be acceptable would it? That's what it's like. You should just say …

MOTHER: What? I can't talk now. My husband, who I talk to for at least ten hours a day, is finishing a point?

FATHER: Just tell them you're busy.

MOTHER: I'm not busy.

FATHER: Oh thank you very much.

MOTHER: Michael we live with each other. We can talk to each other all the time.

FATHER: No we can't, that's the whole point. We work all day, there's Jessica, there's everything else, then you've got work to do in the evening, sometimes I've got work to do in the evening. I mean we do not talk to each other for ten hours a day. Not even ... not even ... *(He does a mental calculation.)* Not even four, really.

MOTHER: I've never met a man who wants to talk so much. Talk talk talk talk talk, all the time.

FATHER: This is a marriage.

MOTHER: Yes, but you didn't contract a permanent companion.

FATHER: That is the definition of marriage.

MOTHER: I mean you even talk to me when I'm on the toilet.

FATHER: Oh I'm sorry. I thought that was a special intimacy that we shared.

MOTHER: Everyone does it! I've got Jessica telling me about her homework while I'm trying to poo, Michael.

FATHER: Jessica does it?

Beat.

MOTHER: Michael. I can't be your special friend all the time.

FATHER: Why not?

MOTHER: I do need some time to myself.

FATHER: You do have time to yourself.

MOTHER: When?

FATHER: On the way to work. At work. At lunch with all of your lawyer friends. Sitting all together in the sun eating ridiculously overpriced sandwiches and discussing who's in, who's out, and whatever else is new on the Rialto. Don't you? Every day.

MOTHER: Michael, I'm allowed other friends. You have friends.

FATHER: Not that are just mine.

MOTHER: You do, Michael.

FATHER: Very few.

MOTHER: What about Lewis?

FATHER: That's one.

MOTHER: And Eric.

FATHER: I never see him.

MOTHER: That's not my fault. He lives in Hawaii.

FATHER: Anyway, I think of them as our friends.

MOTHER: Well they're not. I have absolutely nothing in common with them.

FATHER: You get along very well with Lewis …

MOTHER: I think he drinks too much. But he's your friend. And I don't mind. Be friends with Lewis. Go away on special weekends to Jazz festivals in New Orleans with Lewis. Something I don't do with my friends. But please, just occasionally, would you let me speak to them on the telephone?

FATHER: I went away for one weekend.

MOTHER: The same weekend the dishwasher broke. It was a nightmare.

FATHER: Alright. I have Lewis. But you have lots of people.

MOTHER: I need lots of people, Michael. It's something I need. You don't like most people.

FATHER: I like you.

MOTHER: I know. And I like you.

Beat.

But now I have to work.

She picks up her papers. She starts reading them. Silence. The FATHER checks his watch. She notices. He shrugs helplessly.

FATHER: We don't want to be late …

She throws them down. She gets up and begins to get ready. Silence.

MOTHER: I hate these things. I really don't want to go.

FATHER: It will only take a couple of hours.

MOTHER: I'm working when we get back.

FATHER: Right.

MOTHER: And you're not to interrupt me.

FATHER: Judy, I go out of my way to accommodate you working. It's just that right before a Parent Teacher Conference isn't the best time, is it? You spent an hour with Jessica. And now we have to go.

MOTHER: I wouldn't have been with Jessica for an hour if you hadn't screamed at her.

FATHER: I wouldn't have screamed at her if she wasn't so incredibly badly behaved.

MOTHER: Screaming at her doesn't do anything.

FATHER: I'd have screamed some more if I'd known she spent the afternoon trespassing. Instead of telling her it was fine.

MOTHER: I didn't tell her it was fine.

FATHER: You shouldn't have gone in there at all. She was supposed to be in trouble. That child is getting completely out of control.

MOTHER: No she's not.

FATHER: Oh come on, Judy. Even the other parents want to talk to us about her.

MOTHER: One woman. One parent.

FATHER: Who next? One very angry homeowner who wants to know why she's crushed all of his fucking daffodils? And all you do is sit at the end of her bed swapping secrets for an hour.

MOTHER: I think it's better than losing my temper every five minutes.

FATHER: You shout at Jessica.

MOTHER: Not like you do. You hit her.

FATHER: I occasionally spank her and you do too.

MOTHER: Hardly ever.

FATHER: Because you don't have the energy. So I have to fucking deal with it. And then you throw it back in my face and act as though I were some terrible monster.

MOTHER: No I don't. But I have to put a considerable amount of energy into convincing Jessica that you aren't!

FATHER: That's very good of you. Much appreciated.

MOTHER: You scare her Michael.

FATHER: Well tough eggs! When a fucking tank rolls over me I'm not going to lie down!

MOTHER: I'll tell you what she does when you're shouting at her. She says to herself over and over again 'it doesn't matter.'

FATHER: What?

MOTHER: That's what she told me.

FATHER: No respect for me. It's amazing.

Beat.

Well that explains a lot.

MOTHER: It's a coping strategy.

FATHER: It explains why she just stood there staring at me with this big 'fuck you' look in her eyes.

MOTHER: That's exactly what I'd be thinking if someone called me a tank.

FATHER: You're not a tank. She is.

MOTHER: Which earrings?

FATHER: Those ones.

MOTHER: Michael, she does respect you.

FATHER: That song was pretty nasty, Judy.

MOTHER: We both agreed it wasn't any good at all.

FATHER: She thinks her father's stupid and a monster.

MOTHER: She doesn't, Michael. I explained to her that you're tense about the book.

FATHER: Oh right, I see, you think tonight was my fault.

MOTHER: I think you overreacted.

FATHER: Is that what the two of you were whispering about? My multiple failings? No wonder you took so long.

MOTHER: No, I just told her that the two of you had very different personalities.

FATHER: She's ten. Are you seriously telling me she's right?

MOTHER: You overreact, Michael. You sent her to her room for beating you at Clue!

FATHER: That is not why I sent her to her room and you know it!

MOTHER: You overreacted.

FATHER: Then why didn't you say anything?

MOTHER: Because you told me to keep out of it! I am not supposed to undermine you in front her!

FATHER: You do undermine me! You go straight in there and leave me sitting on the sofa like a fucking lemon.

MOTHER: She was upset!

FATHER: She knew she was way out of line. Until you told her it was all my fault.

MOTHER: I didn't!

FATHER: What about supporting me?

MOTHER: I'm not supporting anyone.

FATHER: I'm glad that's out in the open.

MOTHER: If I want to spend quality time with Jessica on the night of her Parent Teacher Conference then I will. What are you going to do about it?

FATHER: You know if you keep pretending that you and Jessica have a special relationship that doesn't include me, then you and Jessica will have a special relationship that doesn't include me.

MOTHER: It's impossible to talk to you when you're like this.

FATHER: You see? This is what you're like in conflict. You give up.

MOTHER: Michael. I'm a lawyer. My job is conflict.

FATHER: Yes, I know you're very good at your job dear but when it comes to –

MOTHER: Don't you dare!

FATHER: It doesn't help anything if you hide away with Jessica!

MOTHER: We weren't hiding. You could have come in.

FATHER: She didn't want me there!

MOTHER: What did you expect?

FATHER: I expected you to come back out! I had poured us both a glass of wine! You've got time for Ken, you've got time for Jessica, I'm just who you fit in between telephone calls!

MOTHER: That's not true.

FATHER: It is true! The priorities are work, Jessica, me.

MOTHER: Why do you have to put it in an order like that? That's not how it works.

FATHER: Because everything has an order. Everyone has priorities. And I am not yours. Do you ever wish you could spend more time with me?

MOTHER: Michael, we –

FATHER: I wish I could spend more time with you. Every day. And if I could, you wouldn't want it, would you?

MOTHER: I would if I didn't have anything else to do.

FATHER: Oh that's very comforting.

MOTHER: Oh Michael. Come on. I love you.

Pause.

Come on. I love you.

Beat.

I love you.

Beat.

Don't I?

Beat.

Yes I do. You're who I come home to.

FATHER: No, you come home to -

MOTHER: No. In here. You're who I come home to.

Beat.

FATHER: Yes?

MOTHER: Of course. But you have to know that. I can't perform it for you all the time.

FATHER: You're not going to leave me for Ken then?

MOTHER: Don't be absurd.

FATHER: Maybe I could marry Lisa. Who'd get Jessica?

MOTHER: Jessica loves you very much. You know that. Of course she's impossible. She's your daughter.

The FATHER smiles.

But sometimes she can be very sweet, can't she?

FATHER: Yes.

MOTHER: And she's very bright.

FATHER: And freakishly good at Clue.

MOTHER: She'll be alright.

She looks at herself in the mirror.

FATHER: You're beautiful.

MOTHER: Thank you.

FATHER: Are you ready?

MOTHER: I'm ready.

Beat.

Now, you realize we're going to have to think of something to say to Sarah Barnes's mother about the books.

FATHER: We'll think in the car.

MOTHER: Good.

FATHER: Now don't be nervous.

MOTHER: I'm not nervous. Be polite.

FATHER: Judy, would you please remember that it's not us they're assessing.

Beat.

MOTHER: Switch off the light.

They exit, turning out the light.

Act Two

A few hours later. Quiet in the bedroom for a moment. Then the parents return.

MOTHER: Would you just keep your voice down? Jessica's asleep.

FATHER: No I won't keep my fucking voice down. This is outrageous.

MOTHER: I know.

FATHER: I still cannot believe the way that teacher spoke to us. Have you ever heard anything like it?

MOTHER: No. No I haven't.

FATHER: She was so patronizing. 'If you'd just calm down for a moment ...' Calm down. Telling me to calm down. After insulting us.

MOTHER: Well insulting me, actually.

FATHER: Both of us. I think it's unbelievable. How old was she? Twenty-three? I will be writing a letter. Tomorrow. I think it's very interesting that they wouldn't let us see the principal tonight!

MOTHER: He wasn't there.

FATHER: Well he should have been there!

The FATHER looks at her.

Are you alright? What can I get you?

MOTHER: No I'm not alright.

FATHER: I'm going to kill Jessica.

MOTHER: Michael, that's not going to help.

FATHER: This is outrageous. Look at you.

MOTHER: Do I look white?

FATHER: You do.

MOTHER: I went white. When she said it I felt myself go completely white. Did you see?

FATHER: I thought you handled it so well.

MOTHER: Really?

FATHER: Yes. Phenomenally well.

MOTHER: I did stay very calm.

FATHER: You were amazingly calm. I thought I was going to kill her.

MOTHER: So did I.

FATHER: No, but you were amazing. Just got us out of there.

MOTHER: What are we going to do?

FATHER: We're going to talk to Jessica.

MOTHER: I want to talk to her by myself.

FATHER: Oh no. I want to talk to her.

MOTHER: Will you please let me handle this?

FATHER: No. I think we should handle this together.

MOTHER: No, you'll just shout at her.

FATHER: Damn right I'll shout at her. I won't have her talk that way about you.

MOTHER: I'm talking to her by myself.

FATHER: Absolutely not. Not this time.

MOTHER: I need to.

FATHER: No. You'll just let her walk all over you. I won't have it! She's in big trouble.

MOTHER: All she said was "I never see my mother."

FATHER: Yes and it's a fucking lie!

MOTHER: It's a lie, isn't it?

FATHER: You spend more than enough time with Jessica.

MOTHER: Well then why would she say it? I don't understand it.

FATHER: You want to know the reason? I can picture it exactly. She's in trouble at school. She's ... I don't know, talked back, lied, done something. The teachers don't understand it. They take her aside. What a wonderful opportunity to put their amateur psychology to the test! They talk to her very seriously. "Jessica, what's wrong? Is everything alright at home?" And she sees – "aha! This is a way to get out of it."

MOTHER: Do you think so?

FATHER: Oh yes. They probably suggested it. "Do you spend enough time with your mother?" Wouldn't even consider asking about the father, the sexist pigs.

MOTHER: But what if it's not that?

FATHER: It is that. Don't you buy into this. You spend plenty of time with Jessica.

MOTHER: That's not what the school thinks.

FATHER: How the hell would they know?

MOTHER: Because they're with her all day!

FATHER: Everyone at that school is a total idiot.

MOTHER: Look, if Jessica really feels I neglect her then we've got a very big problem.

FATHER: Oh I don't believe this ...

MOTHER: And I want to find out what it is without you standing there glaring at her the whole time.

Beat.

FATHER: Judy …

MOTHER: What?

FATHER: You have got to stop pandering to her.

MOTHER: What do you mean?

FATHER: You have got to stop pandering to her. I'm serious, Judy. That child will take and take and take until there's no more to give. And we have got to stop it. Now.

MOTHER: Well what am I supposed to do! Just let her hate me?

FATHER: She doesn't hate you.

MOTHER: Yes she does. Why else would she say it?

FATHER: Because she loves you. She wants you all the time. Remember when she was a baby? She'd cry every time you left the room for God's sake.

MOTHER: We don't know that's why she was crying.

FATHER: Oh please. It was obvious.

MOTHER: To you.

FATHER: This is the same thing. It's the same fucking thing all over again. She's not a baby anymore. She's a lot fucking smarter. This is just a tactic Judy. It's another tactic to get her own fucking way and I won't stand for it!

Pause.

MOTHER: But why is she like that? *(She is really asking.)* What have we done?

Beat.

FATHER: We haven't done anything.

MOTHER: Well obviously, Michael, we're doing something wrong because it is not normal for a ten-year-old child to

go to her teachers and say she doesn't spend enough time
with her mother! There's a problem!

FATHER: Yes, I think we do have a problem.

MOTHER: What is it?

FATHER: The problem is that our daughter is an attention-
seeking little bitch!

MOTHER: Would you just keep your voice down?

FATHER: I don't give a shit if she hears me! I'm much more
concerned about you.

Beat.

MOTHER: I try to be a good mother …

FATHER: You are a good mother.

MOTHER: Well apparently you're the only one who thinks so.

FATHER: Come on, Judy. You're wonderful with Jessica.

MOTHER: I do the best I can.

FATHER: Of course you do.

MOTHER: That's what I'll say. That I do the best I can. And it's
not easy.

FATHER: I cannot believe they're sending over a social worker.

MOTHER: This is a nightmare.

FATHER: And you don't want me to shout at her. Unbelievable.

MOTHER: It won't help.

FATHER: Why the hell did you tell them it was alright to send
this woman over? I thought it was just a suggestion.

MOTHER: What was I supposed to say? We're not going to
look very good if we refuse to see her.

FATHER: Effectively, our daughter … our daughter, has informed on us. And now they're sending the fucking authorities over. I mean this is fucking Kafka.

MOTHER: Then we'd better clean. Oh look! Some one's getting what they want.

FATHER: We're not cleaning.

MOTHER: I'll have to call the office first thing. I'm going to have to cancel a meeting. Two meetings. The timing couldn't actually be worse.

FATHER: I think we should call her up and tell her Monday isn't convenient.

MOTHER: No.

FATHER: Why?

MOTHER: Because it will look bad.

FATHER: Who gives a shit?

MOTHER: I do.

FATHER: Judy, listen to me. We haven't done anything wrong. We are under no obligation to impress this woman.

MOTHER: Yes we are. So do me a favour Michael and keep your temper when she comes over.

FATHER: Judy this is all a misunderstanding. It will be fine.

Beat.

Come on. You're just tired and you're upset.

MOTHER: Yes I am upset. I'm very upset.

FATHER: Me too.

MOTHER: I don't see why. You're not the one that's in trouble.

FATHER: Judy …

MOTHER: I mean how could this happen?

Beat.

I think she's angry I don't pick her up from school.

FATHER: You do pick her up. We pick her up all the time. Anyway it's only half an hour's walk with Anne-Marie for fuck's sake.

MOTHER: I spend all my time with her. I spend all the time I've got.

FATHER: I know.

MOTHER: I was in there tonight. I was in there for an hour. You got angry with me.

FATHER: I know.

MOTHER: I don't know what else to do. I play with her, I talk to her, I listen to her. I listen to her all the time.

FATHER: I know.

MOTHER: I just don't know what I've done wrong.

FATHER: You haven't done anything wrong.

MOTHER: My mother will be delighted.

FATHER: What's your mother got to do with anything?

MOTHER: It's what she always used to say to me. 'How will you ever manage to bring up a child?' I'm not telling her. I'm not fucking telling her.

FATHER: You're wonderful with Jessica.

MOTHER: You do not mention this to my parents.

FATHER: I won't.

MOTHER: Or anyone.

FATHER: I won't.

MOTHER: What if she says the same thing to this social worker?

FATHER: You think she's going to do that? With us in the house?

MOTHER: I don't know if we can be there while they talk to her.

FATHER: Of course we're going to be there. I'm not leaving my daughter alone with some woman we've never met before who probably gets a bonus every time she sticks a child in a home.

MOTHER: Well what if we have to?

FATHER: Then we should talk to Jessica before she sees her.

MOTHER: What should we say?

FATHER: We'll find out why she said what she said, tell her as a result someone's coming over on Monday who wants to put her in a home and explain that if she says it again that's where she'll end up.

MOTHER: We can't say that.

FATHER: Why not? It's the truth.

MOTHER: Because we can't do that.

FATHER: She has to learn that what she says has consequences. That this isn't the fucking movies!

MOTHER: I have got to find out what's happening to her.

FATHER: Let's talk to her tonight.

MOTHER: I'm talking to her, by myself, tomorrow.

FATHER: She's my daughter too.

MOTHER: I don't care! I'm not going to be able to get anything out of her if you're there.

FATHER: Why the hell not?

MOTHER: Because she's scared of you.

FATHER: No she's not.

MOTHER: She is! She thinks you're going to spank her every five minutes!

FATHER: You're crazy …

MOTHER: It's true.

FATHER: Bullshit. She just knows I don't let her get away with murder.

MOTHER: Well I'm sick of it.

FATHER: You're sick of it? Really?

Beat.

Well I won't stop her next time she bothers you when you're trying to work.

MOTHER: Fine.

FATHER: And you can make sure that she does her homework.

MOTHER: I do.

FATHER: Oh and she really listens to you. Do you know how many times a day I have to say 'listen to your mother'?

MOTHER: You just take over! You never give me a chance to discuss anything with her.

FATHER: It's not up for discussion. She has to do her homework.

MOTHER: You know, if you didn't scare her all the time it's quite possible that none of this would be happening.

FATHER: What?

MOTHER: What? You think this has nothing to do with you?

FATHER: Hey, the school is being ridiculous.

MOTHER: If she's unhappy at home it's not just because of me.

FATHER: She isn't unhappy at home but even if she was, I don't think it's very nice, Judy, to turn around and blame it all on me.

MOTHER: Well why should I be the one that takes all the blame!

FATHER: We haven't done anything. Neither of us have done anything.

MOTHER: Michael. It doesn't matter if we think we haven't done anything. What matters is that she feels she doesn't –

FATHER: She's ten years old.

MOTHER: So what?

FATHER: So what she feels is not an adult perspective.

MOTHER: Did you ever think that the reason that she said she doesn't spend enough time with me, is because she wants to get away from you?

Beat.

FATHER: Judy. That is really hurtful.

MOTHER: Well?

FATHER: No, I didn't think that at all.

MOTHER: Well I think it's perfectly possible.

FATHER: Why?

MOTHER: Because I know my daughter.

FATHER: Oh grow up! This is all just a competition. A competition about who can win.

MOTHER: Win what?

FATHER: Win whatever. What we eat for dinner, what we talk about while we're eating it, what we do when we've finished eating it. Win, win, win, that's all she wants. And you give into her every time.

MOTHER: What would you like me to do? Ignore her?

FATHER: It might be a start. Yes.

MOTHER: Then I'd have plenty of time for you.

FATHER: Oh I doubt the time you saved would go towards me. But I'm sure your clients would benefit hugely. You might make senior partner.

MOTHER: Well perhaps if I concentrated on work a little more, then you could concentrate on work a little more, instead of just sitting around the house criticizing everyone.

FATHER: Fuck you!

MOTHER: Michael!

FATHER: You have no idea how hard I'm working. I work my ass off in ways that you don't understand. That you don't begin to understand, that you don't try to understand.

MOTHER: Fine.

FATHER: I am working all the time, every day.

MOTHER: Then where's the book, Michael?

FATHER: Just because I don't write it down every second.

MOTHER: You don't write it down, no book.

FATHER: You want to do it? You want to write a novel? I'll do your job. I could have been a lawyer. And I'm sure that I, at least, would manage not to lose my files.

MOTHER: I don't want to write a novel, Michael. You do. Don't take it out on me just because you can't do it.

FATHER: I can do it.

MOTHER: Then where's the book?

FATHER: I'll write you a book.

MOTHER: Good. Get going.

FATHER: I'll write you a book and you won't like what's in it.

MOTHER: And I'll have you in court so fast it'll make your head spin, and believe me you'll be writing your next one living alone in some God-forsaken apartment you can barely afford unless you shut the fuck up!

A moment.

FATHER: I would love to see you manage without me. The dishwasher breaks, you call me in fucking tears.

Beat.

What the fuck was I supposed to do about it from New Orleans!

MOTHER: I have to get up early. I'm going to bed.

FATHER: Oh, yes, go to bed. Mustn't be late for the office.

MOTHER: Oh for God's sake, Michael. What do you want me to do? Stay home all day? Is that what you'd like?

A moment.

Is it? Is that what you and Jessica want?

FATHER: No.

MOTHER: Good! Because I won't do it!

FATHER: No one's saying don't work.

MOTHER: It's my job, Michael.

FATHER: You just want to make senior partner.

MOTHER: Of course I want to make senior partner. What's wrong with that? Wouldn't you? When you were writing your first book I hardly saw you.

FATHER: That was years ago.

MOTHER: And I hardly saw you. And I didn't mind.

FATHER: I bet you didn't.

MOTHER: I understood.

FATHER: I understand.

MOTHER: You just don't like it. When you were writing your novel, properly writing it, I loved it. I loved supporting you, and bringing you dinner at your desk, and I felt like you were doing it for both of us.

FATHER: I was.

MOTHER: But you don't feel that way about me.

FATHER: You're not doing it for both of us.

MOTHER: Neither were you.

Beat.

FATHER: No one is more supportive of you that I am. I spend hours helping you draft statements, don't I? And we talk about your cases, and, my God, if it wasn't for me you wouldn't have even applied for the job. It was me who told you to go for the fucking thing.

MOTHER: Then why don't you let me do it?

FATHER: Because you disappear off into this little world that I helped you build and then suddenly I'm not allowed in. And I don't like it. I don't like feeling that there are parts of the day that I am not allowed to make contact with you.

MOTHER: I'm working. It's normal to leave me alone. That is how the rest of the world functions. Why, during every step of the day, are you testing whether or not you are the most important thing in my life?

FATHER: Because I need to know.

MOTHER: Well if you don't know by now ... I mean it's exhausting, Michael. It is absolutely exhausting. If you'd just finish -

FATHER: Finish the book, finish the book. I can't! I can't get Helena over to Portugal!

Beat.

MOTHER: Michael, you can.

Silence.

I'll talk to Jessica before I leave tomorrow morning. I'd be grateful if you didn't upset her about this before school.

FATHER: I love Jessica.

Beat.

I'll make it very clear to the social worker how much I love her. How's that?

MOTHER: Perfect.

FATHER: And we'll make sure the house is very clean, and we'll set you and Jessica in the kitchen by the stove, perhaps you could be braiding her hair, and I'll be very friendly, and you'll be charming, and we'll tell her how I read to Jessica and you sing to her, and Jessica can draw the woman some indecipherable pictures, and then off she'll go, never to be seen again. We'll pass with flying colors.

MOTHER: I don't think it will be quite that simple.

FATHER: Yes it will. If necessary I'll flirt. *(No reaction.)* Judy, it will be fine. Won't it? You know it will be fine.

MOTHER: I ought to tell them, Michael. About the hitting.

FATHER: Stop calling it that!

MOTHER: The spanking.

FATHER: Why?

MOTHER: Because it's relevant.

FATHER: To what?

MOTHER: To the situation.

FATHER: There's no situation. This is a mistake.

MOTHER: I think it's the right thing to do.

FATHER: How is it the right thing to do?

MOTHER: Well because you do hit her –

FATHER: I don't hit her, for Christ's sake -

MOTHER: And I think it affects Jessica's behavior.

FATHER: I'm sorry. I want to get this exactly straight. You're going to tell her, or wait and see if it comes up?

MOTHER: I imagine she'll ask.

FATHER: And what are you going to say?

MOTHER: Well nothing really. I'll just confirm that Jessica's not lying.

FATHER: But I don't think it's something you should bring up.

MOTHER: I think she should know.

FATHER: Why?

MOTHER: Because we all might benefit from talking some things through. This is an opportunity.

FATHER: To what?

MOTHER: To sort out our problems.

FATHER: What problems do we have? What problems did we have before tonight?

MOTHER: Look. Jessica's obviously not happy, I'm not happy.

FATHER: What do you mean you're not happy? You were happy before.

MOTHER: Let's just talk to this woman.

FATHER: I don't want to talk to this woman. I want to talk to you.

MOTHER: Michael, I've worked with social workers and they are usually very intelligent -

FATHER: Oh please.

MOTHER: Some are.

FATHER: I don't like people who's entire careers are built around where to allocate blame!

MOTHER: I'm going to tell her, Michael. I'm sorry.

Pause.

FATHER: On Monday morning, you're going to tell the social worker coming round to investigate our family, that I'm an unfit parent.

MOTHER: No I'm not.

FATHER: Oh yes you are. Because by telling her you're telling somebody who will immediately interpret it as that.

MOTHER: You haven't done anything you're ashamed of. Why are you so worried?

FATHER: Because if you bring it up then it will immediately have more significance than it actually has, won't it? And if Jessica's behavior is anything to go by, she will relish the opportunity to recount countless tales in which I lock her in the closet and beat her with an enormous stick.

MOTHER: I'll say she's lying.

FATHER: How do you know they'll believe you?

MOTHER: You really don't have any faith in the legal system, do you?

FATHER: Not enough to want to go on trial.

Beat.

MOTHER: Trials exist for a reason.

Beat.

FATHER: Hey guess what? I was going to back you up.

MOTHER: About what?

FATHER: They're coming here to talk about you, remember?

MOTHER: Well I'll tell them the truth.

FATHER: How about I tell them the truth?

MOTHER: You should tell them the truth.

FATHER: Alright. I'll tell them the reason Jessica is attention-seeking is that you have no attention to give to any of us.

MOTHER: Fine. You do that.

FATHER: That maybe Jessica feels like I do, every day. Second best.

MOTHER: You tell her, Michael.

FATHER: You're obsessed with your work!

MOTHER: Fine. Let it play itself out.

FATHER: And you spend no time with her at all!

MOTHER: If you do that I'll tell the social worker you beat the shit out of her.

Silence.

FATHER: I presume you want this to play itself out so that the two of us are still left with Jessica?

MOTHER: Yes.

FATHER: Right. Then why tell her anything at all? *(No response.)* You've never brought this up before. *(No response.)* I'll tell you what. I'll stop. She won't. You take over. What do you want to do with her the next time?

MOTHER: She'll have to go to her room.

FATHER: Great. You send her.

MOTHER: I will.

FATHER: And I'll sneak up in there with her and the two of us will have a secret little conference, like we're in a gang!

MOTHER: I can stop her allowance.

FATHER: I doubt she'd prefer that. More points for me.

MOTHER: It's not about what she'd prefer.

FATHER: Isn't it? I thought that's what all of this was about. What Jessica wants.

MOTHER: No. It's about what's best for her.

FATHER: And you think that's locking her up. Fine with me. We'll try it.

MOTHER: Look, I don't know! I don't know, Michael! How am I supposed to know? But someone's coming over and I think they might be of help. We sit down, we have a conversation and we sort it out.

FATHER: What makes you think they're on our side?

MOTHER: Well who's side do you think they're on?

FATHER: They're on the side of right. And if there's one thing we've learned about 'right,' it's that it isn't objective. In real life, right and wrong is not the preserve of one person or another. These people aren't interested in you, and they aren't interested in me, and they aren't interested in Jessica. They're interested in their own power, that they've built on their own fucking moral high-ground. And they are going to come in here and make pronouncements on a situation that they know next to nothing about –

MOTHER: But I want to know! I want to know, Michael!

Beat.

FATHER: You want to know what?

MOTHER: I want to know if I'm doing it right.

FATHER: How the hell are they going to know that?

MOTHER: They'll talk to Jessica. They'll talk to us. They're trained, Michael.

FATHER: What, in absolute truth?

127

MOTHER: They might not make pronouncements! It might just be suggestions.

FATHER: If there was a perfect way to bring up a child don't you think that someone might have published it in a little manual?

MOTHER: There's lots of different types of children.

FATHER: Oh I'm sure this woman has whittled it down to two categories: those who should be with their parents, and those who shouldn't.

MOTHER: It's not going to come down to that.

FATHER: How do you know? If you start this ball rolling who knows where it will end?

MOTHER: I know exactly where it will end. I'm white, I'm middle class and I earn in the upper tax bracket. Nobody's taking my daughter anywhere.

FATHER: Then why do this?

MOTHER: Because I need some support.

FATHER: Rallying the troops against me? Getting the army into position?

MOTHER: No Michael.

FATHER: I mean for God's sake, Judy! What do you want? Is this to punish me? To discipline me? Is that what you want? Little Michael to get the back of his legs slapped by a social worker? Is that what it will take for you to know that you're right?

MOTHER: Michael. Calm down.

FATHER: They won't stop with me. They'll move on to you. Are you ready for that?

MOTHER: They can't hurt us.

FATHER: Are you ready to listen to them tell you that perhaps you shouldn't have let me spank Jessica if you didn't like it?

MOTHER: I'm ready to listen.

FATHER: Listen to them tell you that Jessica would probably be happier if you were home all the time? Listen to them tell you that perhaps applying for senior partner at this evidently unsettling time for Jessica might not be the best thing for her psycho-social development?

MOTHER: If it's the right thing to do.

FATHER: And you'll do what they say?

MOTHER: That's not what I said. I said I would listen to what they had to say.

FATHER: Oh no. If we bring someone else in, there's no going back.

MOTHER: What's that supposed to mean?

FATHER: How seriously are you going to take them? What if they tell you I've been a bad father? What then? Will you divorce me? Or just throw it in my face every time we have a fight?

MOTHER: But you're not a bad father.

FATHER: They'll think you're just defending me, Judy.

MOTHER: Michael, they might tell us we're doing just fine. Imagine that. Can you imagine the relief?

Beat.

They're there anyway. They're watching anyway. The school is, now whoever they're sending. Let's just say what's been going on.

FATHER: How we bring up our child is about us. What matters is what you think. And what I think. Not what they think. This is a family. We're the authority. We make the rules.

MOTHER: Michael, I need something bigger than us! I just can't see through all of the discussion anymore.

FATHER: Then think harder.

MOTHER: I want to give them all the details.

Beat.

FATHER: Interesting, isn't it? Language. They. Them. Not us. They're not us.

MOTHER: No.

FATHER: Then I'm not enough for you.

MOTHER: Michael. Please. I'm too tired.

Silence. He looks at her.

FATHER: Would you die for me?

MOTHER: No, I wouldn't.

FATHER: Why?

MOTHER: Someone would have to be there for Jessica.

Beat.

FATHER: If you died for me, I'd be there for Jessica.

Pause.

I'd die for you. I would.

MOTHER: Alright. You look after Jessica, and I'll die for you. Happy?

FATHER: You haven't had to give up a single thing for this marriage, have you?

MOTHER: What?

FATHER: You haven't had to give anything up. And you wouldn't, would you? Not your files. Not your schedule. Not your life.

Pause.

MOTHER: Why should I? Why should either of us?

FATHER: No sense of loss.

MOTHER: We're not meant to lose anything. We're meant to gain. It's meant to be a gain. What do you feel like you've lost?

FATHER: Me. You.

MOTHER: Well we're here, aren't we?

FATHER: The door opens and other people come in to play with their rules and their games. I don't like their games. You do.

MOTHER: This isn't a game.

FATHER: I thought that the idea of marriage was that you built your own little world and it was over. That nobody bothered you anymore. That finally, you could just sit on the grass with your best friend and not be frightened that they were going to go away and make a new best friend, and not be frightened that you'd be left alone on the grass until they both came back again over to where you're sitting and kick your head in. I thought that you'd get to do everything together. That you'd get to enjoy everything together. And face everything together. Alone.

MOTHER: We do –

FATHER: It's funny. I've always known you didn't want that. I'd sense it every so often but I'd ignore it, push it away, or force you into it. I've seen myself, you know, make you give things up, bully you, beg you, beg you for attention. It's humiliating. And I spend nine minutes out of ten trying to force myself not to do it. But I usually lose the struggle. The way I love you I … I look over at you making tea, or reading a book and I feel it charging through my body and I stand very still in case you see, and feel it as desperation. I honestly thought it would go away. After a couple of years. Settle down. But it hasn't. I don't think it ever will.

Beat.

MOTHER: I do love you too, you know?

FATHER: I think that you love me as much as anyone who isn't your flesh. I do. But they are two very different things. We love in two different ways. I can bear it. Most of the time. I can bear it. Most of the time. It's fine.

Silence. The MOTHER doesn't know what to say. The FATHER turns to leave.

I'm going downstairs.

MOTHER: Why?

FATHER: To work for a while.

MOTHER: Well that's good.

FATHER: Yes. Yes it is good, I suppose. I should cancel the painters. We won't want them here on Monday.

MOTHER: Thanks.

The FATHER turns to leave again.

I had an idea in the car. I thought we could ask my sister to give Jessica a few piano lessons before next semester. To see if she likes it.

FATHER: Oh let her play the trumpet if she wants to. Why not?

MOTHER: No, I agree. The piano's better.

FATHER: Sure. Fine.

The FATHER turns to leave again.

MOTHER: Good night.

He exits. The MOTHER sits there alone. She runs out of the room.

All's quiet.

Suddenly, the parents are back. Kissing. Pulling at each others clothes. A desperate attempt to hang on to each other. They get to the bed.

End of play.

THE MYSTERY OF LOVE AND SEX

The Mystery Of Love & Sex was first produced by Lincoln Center Theater (Andre Bishop, Producing Artistic Director; Adam Siegel, Managing Director) at the Mitzi E. Newhouse Theater in New York City on March 2, 2015. The performance was directed by Sam Gold, with sets by Andrew Lieberman, costumes by Kaye Voyce, lights by Jane Cox and sound and composition by Daniel Kluger. The Production Stage Manager was Janet Takami. The cast was as follows:

CHARLOTTE	Gayle Rankin
JONNY	Mamadou Athie
HOWARD	Tony Shaloub
LUCINDA	Diane Lane
HOWARD'S FATHER	Bernie Passeltiner

Characters

Charlotte

Jonny

Howard

Lucinda

Howard's Father

Setting
The play takes place on the outskirts of major cities in the American south.

Time
Act One takes place five years before Act Two.

Author's Notes
Charlotte and her parents, Lucinda and Howard, are Caucasian. Lucinda is a Southerner. Howard is a New York transplant. At the top of the play, Charlotte is twenty-one years old. Jonny is African-American and the same age as Charlotte.

For Ben

Act One

SCENE ONE

Evening. An uninspiring dorm room to which CHARLOTTE and JONNY have tried to add inspiration.

CHARLOTTE, JONNY, LUCINDA and HOWARD stand near a very low table set for dinner. The room feels too small. Everyone is trying.

LUCINDA: Oh my god, it's so cute, it's so *cute*, the way you've done this.

HOWARD: What did you do? You pushed the two tables together?

CHARLOTTE: Right, we pushed the two tables together, the other one's from Jonny's dorm room, and we made one big table, like a dining room table.

HOWARD: Right.

CHARLOTTE: And we covered it with a sheet.

JONNY: I said get a tablecloth.

CHARLOTTE: We put the sheet over the table, thus transforming it into a tablecloth.

JONNY: A sheet on a table is not a tablecloth. Especially when it's flannel.

LUCINDA: I like it, it's Bohemian, isn't that what you were going for? And I love the candles. Are they scented?

JONNY: Yes they are. I got them on discount.

LUCINDA: Vanilla?

JONNY: I think maybe it was papaya? I can check, the container's in the trash.

CHARLOTTE: Honey, it doesn't matter, it's just an "ah" scent, right? Vanill-ah. Papaya-ah. Just *(She inhales and exhales luxuriously.)* Aaaah.

Everyone looks at her.

I just mean, just like, there's no reason to involve the trash. Let's have wine.

JONNY grabs a bottle.

JONNY: Yes. Who wants wine?

CHARLOTTE: We call it the Spanish red. I don't know what its real name is, but we call it the Spanish red.

JONNY: It's Tusca di Torro.

HOWARD: *(Theatrically.)* Ah! Di Torro!

Beat.

JONNY: Exactly.

CHARLOTTE: It's very cheap but it's the *best* of the cheap. That's what I said the first time I went into the liquor store here. I said, "I want your very best cheap wine."

HOWARD: *(To JONNY.)* Shall I open it?

JONNY: Great.

He hands the wine to HOWARD.

And we have wine glasses.

As he goes to get glasses, he and CHARLOTTE pass each other, squeezing past in the limited space.

Sorry, dear.

CHARLOTTE: Excuse me, angel.

JONNY hands a glass to each parent.

HOWARD: And we'll need a corkscrew.

CHARLOTTE: *(To JONNY.)* Shall I sit down? Are you going to serve?

Beat as JONNY assesses the most effective way to host a dinner party.

JONNY: You can sit.

CHARLOTTE sits on the floor by the table, cross-legged. HOWARD is disconcerted.

HOWARD: Are we sitting on the floor?

CHARLOTTE: Yes. Next to the table with the tablecloth. You didn't see that coming?

LUCINDA: I told you! Bohemian.

CHARLOTTE: Stop saying that.

LUCINDA: Sorry.

LUCINDA sits.

Can we smoke in here?

JONNY: It's not that Bohemian.

HOWARD: She's quitting anyway, aren't you, Lula?

LUCINDA: I have seen several hypnotists. To no avail.

HOWARD: You have to want to.

LUCINDA: I don't want to. You want me to. That must be the problem.

JONNY: You know, if everyone sits, I can serve.

HOWARD: It's just my back ...

LUCINDA: I expect it's good for you to sit on a nice hard surface.

CHARLOTTE: Come on, Dad, it's supposed to be fun. It's ... *(Confidence in the evening drains out of her.)* we, don't have a proper table and chairs ...

HOWARD: You have chairs.

HOWARD points to a chair.

CHARLOTTE: I know, but then we have to put food on our laps, and I thought well this is how the Japanese do it, right? So I thought –

JONNY: I said we should eat with our plates on our laps. We still can.

CHARLOTTE: Yeah. Oh course. Let's eat with plates on our lap like old women in front of the TV. Great.

She stands up, knocking the table a little. Beat.

HOWARD: No. If this is how the Japanese do it.

HOWARD sits down next to the table. CHARLOTTE sits down next to him.

Yes, I suppose this makes sense.

JONNY brings over an enormous bowl of salad. Then he sits down. They are all round the table. Pause.

JONNY: Help yourself, Lucinda.

LUCINDA: This looks like the Garden of Eden and I can't wait to eat it.

LUCINDA serves herself salad.

CHARLOTTE: It's all fresh vegetables. We have this thing, when we're giving a dinner party, because like some people try to pretend that they have actual ovens, like we have at home, but we don't here. The dorm kitchens have this weird little machine – what's it called, Jonny?

JONNY: It's a Forman Grill.

LUCINDA: Oh!

Everyone looks at her.

(On the brink of laughter.) I was going to say "Bohemian" again but I didn't. I stopped myself.

Beat.

CHARLOTTE: Anyway, you can't really cook on it and have the food taste good –

JONNY: It doesn't *heat* anything properly.

CHARLOTTE: But some people because they're trying to be grownups and pretend like they have a real kitchen, which is ridiculous –

JONNY: It is. It is ridiculous.

CHARLOTTE: They cook on it. But we have this thing that we *acknowledge* the limited resources. But then work with them. So I was like … *what if we forget the heat?*

JONNY: Exactly.

CHARLOTTE: What is food without *heat*? What would that *be*?

HOWARD: *(Grimly.)* Salad.

CHARLOTTE: Right.

HOWARD: Just salad?

CHARLOTTE: And bread and butter.

HOWARD: Aha!

CHARLOTTE: Except no butter. I forgot to get it.

HOWARD: Just salad, honey?

JONNY: I tried to pick out hefty vegetables.

Silence for a while as the salad finishes making the rounds and begins to be chewed.

LUCINDA: That is a piquant dressing.

CHARLOTTE: Not too much lemon?

LUCINDA: Perfect.

HOWARD: And you squeezed the lemons yourself.

CHARLOTTE: Yes. How did you know?

HOWARD: Here's a seed.

He removes it from his mouth.

LUCINDA: Why are you being such an asshole?

HOWARD: Hey!

LUCINDA: These kids went to a lot of trouble.

HOWARD: They did?

LUCINDA: Yes!

CHARLOTTE: *(At the same time.)* Yes! Jonny, can you please explain the vision behind this meal? We put a lot of thought into it actually.

JONNY: Well ... there are some families for whom this is a delicious, evening meal. Salad and bread. Fresh. Simple. Natural Cuisine. It's very French. That's why we got French bread, see.

HOWARD takes a piece.

HOWARD: Yes, the French love it. They do. Du pain.

He takes a bite of his bread. Chews. Swallows. Everyone relaxes.

You know what else they love? Du Beurre.

Everyone tenses.

(Cheerfully.) But you know who *don't* care about butter? The Japanese. So in a way this all makes sense.

He kisses his daughter on the cheek.

Love you, honey. I'm sorry. I just miss you a lot. Driving here ... Oh, every mile between us was an agony.

LUCINDA: Oh your father outdid himself. Not one speeding ticket. Two.

HOWARD: I explained I was on my way to see my daughter at college who I miss more than life itself. Did they care?

LUCINDA: He explained this to both sets of highway patrol.

HOWARD: I told them, I said my little girl's going to be President of the United States some day and when she is she will hunt you down.

LUCINDA: I begged him to let me do the talking –

HOWARD: Lula, honey –

LUCINDA: You called one of the officers "sir."

HOWARD: I was being polite.

LUCINDA: It was a ma'am. That was your first mistake.

HOWARD: That was not a woman. Maybe it wasn't a man, but it wasn't a woman. Not with those sideburns.

LUCINDA: Honey, I have told you. The minute you open your mouth we have a problem. They hear you weren't born here, a Southern cop is a Southern cop, that makes them hate you. So then they want to see your license. And that is the nail in the coffin, my friend.

JONNY: What's wrong with his license?

HOWARD: Nothing at all.

LUCINDA: It's his last name. Combine it with his face and his accent and what you have is a New York Jew.

HOWARD: So I shouldn't speak?

LUCINDA: Not to highway patrol men. You should let me speak. Fact is my father's name still opens up a lot of doors in this state.

HOWARD: There was a time you wouldn't walk through a door if your father's name opened it.

LUCINDA: I am quite sure I could have gotten Madam Sideburns to relent with or without my daddy's name. But Charlotte, if you really are serious about becoming a politician and running in Georgia then you need to use my last name, not your father's.

HOWARD: I agree with her about that, honey. It will make things easier. Unless you move to New York. Then by all means, go Jew.

CHARLOTTE: I think you're under-estimating the South, but whatever.

HOWARD: Listen there's nothing wrong with changing a name to get ahead. Jews have been doing it for centuries. It's the only way. That is the great advantage Jews have over black people, right Jonny. We can pass. Sometimes we get to pass.

JONNY: Right, and not being brought to America on slave ships in chains from Africa. That was also an advantage.

HOWARD: Absolutely. *(He chews his bread.)* Although there were ships. That we got on, following pogroms. Following death camps. You know what? From now on I am always going to eat bread dry. As a writer it's useful for me to identify with ... everyone. Everyone. And this is definitely giving me an insight into what it might be like to be a homeless person.

JONNY: *(Standing, accidentally knocking the table.)* I'll go get some butter.

LUCINDA: What about some olive oil? We can dip the bread in olive oil. Like Italians.

HOWARD: This is such a cosmopolitan meal. It's almost overwhelming.

JONNY: We're actually out of olive oil. But I'll go get butter. I don't mind.

CHARLOTTE: *(Standing, also accidentally knocking the table.)* No, I will. I'm the one who forgot it. Even though you wrote it down. On the list.

LUCINDA: I will go and purchase butter.

HOWARD: She means go smoke a cigarette. I am not a writer of detective fiction for nothing.

CHARLOTTE: Mom, no cigarettes.

HOWARD: *(To LUCINDA.)* Do the thing the hypnotist told you to do. *(Explaining.)* Whenever she wants to smoke she has to …

He looks at LUCINDA: Do it. LUCINDA gives an exasperated sigh. Then she clicks her fingers and inhales very deeply.

I'm really proud of you, Lula-belle.

LUCINDA: I'm putting myself through this for you. Make no mistake about that.

HOWARD kisses her. During his kiss she makes the decision to kiss him back. This all takes a few seconds. During this, CHARLOTTE indicates to JONNY that the kissing is unfortunate but beyond her control.

JONNY: *(To CHARLOTTE.)* I'll get butter. You visit with your parents. They're here to see you.

CHARLOTTE: OK. Do you have money, angel?

JONNY: Back in a sec.

JONNY exits.

LUCINDA: His mom has a care package for him. Remind me. It's in the car.

CHARLOTTE: Dad, can we not do the Jew versus Black thing.

HOWARD: What Jew versus Black thing?

CHARLOTTE: You know. Who had it worse?

LUCINDA: Agree, that is a bad topic.

HOWARD: *(Baffled.)* That is a topic I neither raised nor discussed.

CHARLOTTE is about to disagree but – without HOWARD seeing – LUCINDA indicates she should leave it alone.

(With cheer.) Hey! I have something for you!

He holds out a scrap of paper.

CHARLOTTE: What is that?

LUCINDA: Oh Jesus …

HOWARD: This is the cell phone number of one Scott Harris. You may have heard of him. He has won an Emmy. And stars as the brooding bastard son of Detective Grayson in the slightly dubious TV adaptation of my books. He wants to meet you.

CHARLOTTE: Why?

HOWARD: I may have shown him your picture.

CHARLOTTE: Why would I want to meet him?

HOWARD: He's a movie star! Regular people can't get his number. Here is his number. Take it. *(He pushes the scrap of paper into her hand.)* Just think about it. He's special.

LUCINDA: That's a tiny little bed they have you sleeping on here. Has it seen much action?

HOWARD: Lucinda!

CHARLOTTE: *(At the same time.)* Mom!

LUCINDA: *(To HOWARD.)* I am trying to find out in a subtle way.

CHARLOTTE: Nothing subtle is happening here.

HOWARD: *(To LUCINDA.)* I think it's best to be direct. Like this. *(To CHARLOTTE.)* Are you and Jonny together now?

CHARLOTTE: *(Beat.)* Why do you want to know?

LUCINDA: We're curious, honey. The two of you seem … *closer* … than usual.

HOWARD: I mean, you don't have to tell us, of course. But we don't like secrets. And the two of you appear to have all but set up house so … I'm a fan of clarity, is all.

Suddenly, the atmosphere is serious.

CHARLOTTE: We are not dating. Not … like … officially. I mean … like …

HOWARD: Enough with the "like." Why can't you kids ever just say what is happening? Why is there always this approximation? What *is* it? On its own terms?

CHARLOTTE: I don't know what it is! We've known each other since we were nine. We are very much beyond "dating." In the conventional sense. But … yeah, I mean it's serious. We're serious. I can't live without him. That kind of thing.

HOWARD: Jonny's mom said something about the two of you moving in together.

CHARLOTTE: We're definitely moving in together after we graduate. He's coming to D.C. with me.

HOWARD: To do what?

CHARLOTTE: A Master's at Georgetown.

HOWARD: He won't get into Georgetown.

CHARLOTTE: What do you know about his grades?

HOWARD: I remember what they were in high school.

CHARLOTTE: He's very smart.

HOWARD sighs heavily.

CHARLOTTE: Oh, don't do the sigh, Dad.

HOWARD: I think we should discuss this. In more detail. Later.

CHARLOTTE: Why? I *love* Jonny. You know that. You guys do too! He practically grew up in our house.

HOWARD: The whole point of college is to experiment. What's that song? *(Loudly.)* From *Bee!* To *Bee!* To *Bee!*

LUCINDA: Is he drunk?

HOWARD: It's from *The King and I.* You've got to cross-pollinate and explore your options. There are a lot of men out there. In the blink of an eye, you'll be married. Don't make a mistake.

LUCINDA: What the hell is that, the voice of experience?

CHARLOTTE: You took against Jonny because of the egg whites.

HOWARD: No, but I'll tell you what. The egg whites was a character detail that said *everything*. I write characters, that is what I do, and if I wrote a character that only ate the yolk of a boiled egg and not the outside I would intend the reader to draw conclusions from that. Because it implies taking the easy road.

CHARLOTTE: *(Through gritted teeth.)* It *implies* he doesn't like egg whites.

HOWARD: Who care's if he likes them! It was a meal we cooked for him and it was impolite! It was indicative of character, Charlotte! As is a straight C student in high school who did not participate in a single after-school activity –

CHARLOTTE: That's not him, that's how he was *raised*. He wasn't pushed. His mother –

HOWARD: Jonny's mother does not approve of this. She is a committed Baptist, Charlotte. She doesn't want a Jewish daughter-in-law, I don't care how sweet she is to you. And on the subject of the boy's mother –

LUCINDA: FYI the boy is out buying butter and could be back any moment.

CHARLOTTE: Is this because he's black?

HOWARD: *What?*

LUCINDA: She went there. As I told you she would.

HOWARD: Wow.

CHARLOTTE: The boy. That's racist.

HOWARD: That is *Southern* for any underling, the underling in this case being a kid a generation or three below me, who did not come home for Christmas break despite –

CHARLOTTE: He did an exchange with a school in *Finland*. It was a big opportunity –

HOWARD: There are no opportunities in Finland.

CHARLOTTE: That is so American-centric.

HOWARD: He did not come home for Christmas although it might have been his mother's last Christmas.

CHARLOTTE: She's not dying! Jonny says she's doing really well.

HOWARD: She lies to him and he chooses to believe her lies. That is an indication of character. Believe me, she's dying. A man would come home and help her get her damn groceries from the car to the kitchen and spend some time saying goodbye. Believe me. I know. I did it.

LUCINDA: You were forty years old, Howard. Jonny's not even twenty-one. He *is* a boy. They're both just children and this is getting way too serious.

She does her hypnosis cigarette thing again. Father and daughter watch for a second then:

CHARLOTTE: Jonny says his mother is not dying. And I think he would know better than you. *(Beat.)* You like Jonny, don't you Mom?

LUCINDA: *(Non-committal.)* Jonny's a cutie-pie.

CHARLOTTE: You and Dad met in college.

LUCINDA: That's true. A little too young. I never finished my degree and we alienated both of our families but apart from that yes, we are the perfect model.

HOWARD: You admitted in the car she could do better.

LUCINDA: Uh huh, I did. And I also told you they've been in love since they were children.

CHARLOTTE: That's what a marriage is, right? Best friends?

HOWARD: So we are talking about marriage?

CHARLOTTE: That was theoretical. *(Beat.)* Jonny would die if he knew we were talking like this. And he'll be back any second.

CHARLOTTE pours herself more wine.

LUCINDA: I agree. Enough.

CHARLOTTE: Jonny's mom didn't do a *thing* to help him with his studies. She wouldn't pick him up for after school activities.

HOWARD: A bright kid finds a way.

CHARLOTTE: He made it here, didn't he? He's getting a degree.

HOWARD gives an ominous sigh.

(Emphatically.) Let us shelve this. He'll be back soon.

HOWARD: You threw away Yale for this guy.

CHARLOTTE: I threw it away because I have never met a single person who went to Yale that is not an asshole.

HOWARD: I went to Yale.

LUCINDA: So did I. It was an asshole factory.

HOWARD: OK, but can I go back to what I was saying? Forget
Yale. Yale wasn't right. I understand that you are someone
who needs to feel safe. But when we packed up your bags
you were supposed to be going out into the world, not
playing house in a room with a kid from back home.

JONNY enters. HOWARD does not skip a beat.

So I said to my publisher, "Listen, I am not beholden to
you or the American public to continue writing Detective
Grayson. Twenty-seven novels are enough. I'm working on
something new." Hi, Jonny!

JONNY: I have butter! And also some smoked turkey.

HOWARD: Now you're talking! Hand it over.

JONNY hands it to HOWARD.

CHARLOTTE: *(To JONNY.)* I thought we don't do processed
meat.

JONNY: I think your dad wanted some more food.

HOWARD: How'd you guess, Jonny?

JONNY: I just sensed it.

HOWARD: *(Making himself a turkey sandwich.)* Now if only we
had some Swiss cheese … you guys don't have any Swiss
cheese, lying around do you?

CHARLOTTE and JONNY shake their heads.

No matter.

He makes himself a sandwich with gusto.

Mayo?

LUCINDA: Shut up!

JONNY: So listen, Howard. There was a favor I wanted to ask you.

HOWARD: If you go get me some Swiss cheese, the answer is definitely yes.

JONNY half-rises, uncertainly.

CHARLOTTE: *(Firmly.)* He's kidding.

JONNY sits down again.

LUCINDA: What is it, honey?

JONNY: I have to write a final paper this year for English Lit. And I'd like to do it on you. On your work.

LUCINDA: That is so sweet.

CHARLOTTE: I told him you'd be fine with it.

JONNY: It's a big paper. Like, the whole semester's grade basically depends on this paper. And I'm applying to graduate schools for English Lit. So like … it's really important I get a good grade. And I was thinking about Hitchcock. Like, nobody really noticed Hitchcock was a genius. Like, everyone saw his movies. But it wasn't until Truffaut that people understood that Hitchcock wasn't just an entertainer. He was an auteur.

CHARLOTTE: There's a series of interviews Truffaut did with Hitchcock –

HOWARD: Yes, thank you, I understand. I too have been to university.

LUCINDA: You want to interview Howard? Is that what you're saying, honey?

JONNY: Yes. If it's OK. Over spring break.

CHARLOTTE: The last paper he wrote he entered into a student competition, judged by the faculty. He won. Meaning it got, you know, an A. *Plus.*

JONNY is confused, although not displeased, as to why they are discussing his grades.

HOWARD: That is great. Did you tell your mother?

JONNY: No, it just happened.

HOWARD: I'll tell you what. You can interview me over spring break. Take as much time as you need. One condition. You go call your mother right now and tell her about your great success.

JONNY: Well … we're eating dinner, right now.

HOWARD: Your mom is having a tough time, right now. She says she only speaks to you once a week.

LUCINDA: Honey, I think you added the "only."

JONNY: I call her on Sundays when she gets back from church.

HOWARD: She's been too sick to go to church recently. Did she mention that? I know that because I bring her fresh fruit from our tree every week. You want to know the truth, you need to ask the right questions.

LUCINDA: That's a line from one of your books.

HOWARD: *(Irritated.)* No, it's a line that came out of my mouth right now.

LUCINDA: *(Trying to lighten the mood.)* I think it's in one of his books.

Beat.

JONNY: So I'll call her.

JONNY exits.

HOWARD: If he's a contender for son-in-law I will knock him into shape. Butter, please.

LUCINDA: Look, honey. Grandpa died.

CHARLOTTE stares at her.

CHARLOTTE: Are you OK?

LUCINDA: I'm fine, sugar. A little sad. But we hadn't spoken for years, so.

CHARLOTTE: Yeah. *(Beat.)* I mean I don't feel anything really. I only met him a few times. Sorry.

LUCINDA: You don't need to be sorry for not feeling anything. I don't feel anything.

HOWARD: That's not true. Your mother felt a lot. Day of. Didn't you, honey? It's OK to say that.

LUCINDA does her giving-up-smoking-inhalation. She tries to smile through it.

(To CHARLOTTE.) I'm sorry we gave you such a lousy lot of grandparents. honey.

LUCINDA: *(Sharply.)* You adore your father, Howard.

HOWARD: My father is a giant pain in the ass.

LUCINDA: You think everyone is a giant pain in the ass.

HOWARD: I know, I know. The two of you are really the only people I can tolerate.

CHARLOTTE: Tolerate?

CHARLOTTE shoves HOWARD playfully. LUCINDA shoves him in the other direction. They eat in silence for a few moments. A sense of a family portrait. A sense of a loving family.

SCENE TWO

The dorm room, 3am. Shadows and candlelight. CHARLOTTE and JONNY. A mostly-drunk bottle of whiskey.

CHARLOTTE: I don't think they were gracious guests.

JONNY: Your mom was.

CHARLOTTE: Because she a nice Southern girl. But my dad was born, and will always be, a rude New Yorker.

JONNY: A pushy Jew.

CHARLOTTE: Hey.

JONNY: What? You've said it a thousand times. Nothing wrong with being a pushy Jew. Without pushy Jews we wouldn't have Hollywood.

CHARLOTTE: Are you going to say we run the banks too?

JONNY: Your impersonation of my mother would sound totally racist to anyone else. But there is trust here.

CHARLOTTE: *(Her impersonation.)* "Sweet Jesus, I'm full as a tick and that's 'cause I'm blessed."

JONNY: She doesn't *like* to talk on the phone. Your dad doesn't understand. She's not a phone person. She has to come all the way down the stairs to answer. That's how much she isn't a phone person, she doesn't have a phone in her bedroom.

CHARLOTTE: How's she doing?

JONNY: Chemo isn't vey *nice.* But it's shrinking the thing down, so …

CHARLOTTE: The doctors confirmed that?

JONNY: What do you mean?

CHARLOTTE: I know your mom likes to look on the bright side, that's all.

JONNY: She said the doctor said it's shrinking.

CHARLOTTE: That's good.

JONNY: It was really controlling the way your dad did that.

CHARLOTTE: Did what?

JONNY: Made me call her. He's such a *dad.*

CHARLOTTE: I know.

JONNY: If he's not careful I'm going to write a really vicious paper about him.

CHARLOTTE: Don't.

JONNY: Why?

CHARLOTTE: Because he's mine.

JONNY: There's a lot of racism in his books, you know that?

CHARLOTTE: No, I do not know that.

JONNY: Shiny black body. That's a phrase he uses. A lot.

CHARLOTTE: Is that racist?

JONNY: Fetishistic.

CHARLOTTE: It's not fair that it's the same word for fetishism as it is for like ... lynching people. There should be as many words for racism as the Eskimos have for snow.

JONNY: It's all racism.

CHARLOTTE: It's all snow.

JONNY: What he doesn't get is my mom doesn't *want* me seeing her when she's sick like this. She told me very clearly, she's glad I'm not around. She *told* me to apply for the Finnish exchange. I know your dad thinks I should drop out of school and take care of her –

CHARLOTTE: He doesn't. He thinks you should call her more often but that's a cultural thing. That's to do with Jews. And telephones.

JONNY: She's getting good care. The prognosis is good. The doctor said chemo's just a precaution.

CHARLOTTE: How can it be a precaution if it's shrinking the thing?

JONNY: Tell your dad I write to her, letters sometimes. Whenever I see something I think she might appreciate, I write it down and I mail a letter to her. How many sons do that?

CHARLOTTE: What kind of things do you think she'll appreciate?

JONNY: Like ... last spring I saw someone planting crocuses on campus. And they looked real pretty. And they're her favorite flower, so ... I told her about it. And she wrote back, asking about what type of crocuses and what kind of light they were getting and how long they'd last. So I found out the answers from a gardener. And I wrote her what he told me. And it was like this whole exchange we had on paper. And it was really beautiful because it was about her favorite flower. Tell your dad that happened.

CHARLOTTE: You tell him. *(Beat.)* Do you think maybe you should cry?

JONNY: What?

CHARLOTTE: You looked like you were going to cry.

JONNY: I'm not.

CHARLOTTE: You should drink more. Because it can be a release. It's healthy in that way. Like, Bacchanalia. That was necessary, according to Romans, because it was like an organized forum to be insane. Due to drunkenness. Every so often people need to get wasted so they can just let it all go and just fucking feel what they're feeling. And maybe that's joy and maybe that's a profound sadness, but for the Romans, and I agree, it was very necessary to let it out.

JONNY: If I drink more I'll get the hiccups.

CHARLOTTE: You have to push past the hiccups. To the release.

JONNY: Hiccups are embarrassing and make me want to go to home.

CHARLOTTE: But when you're with me, when you're just with me, it's OK. Look, I know I'm a very intense individual. I cry often. I tried to kill myself when I was nine. But I think you're sad too. There's something inside everyone that needs to get out. If you don't let it out, it kills you.

JONNY: What do you think's inside me?

CHARLOTTE: I think you're real sad about your mom. I think you're real sad you never knew your dad, even though you never talk about it.

JONNY: Indeed, I am. I am sad about those things.

Somehow, she awkwardly strokes his hair. He awkwardly lets himself put his head in her lap. All of this is a pause … until:

But that doesn't mean I have anything to say. Sometimes words are so … like most people most of the time are opening and closing their mouths and saying *nothing.*

Beat.

CHARLOTTE: You don't mean me, right?

JONNY: No. But like, pretty much everyone else at this school.

CHARLOTTE: Agreed.

JONNY: Sometimes I think that the only way to be truthful is to say nothing at all.

Silence until they feel certain they are living in a truthful moment together.

CHARLOTTE: Jonny? We're so lucky to have us. I feel like we're this model of how the world should be, you know? I'm a Jewish girl and you're a Christian boy. You're black and I'm white. But when we're together, we're so beyond that. It's so pure. I feel like people should study us.

JONNY: There should totally be a documentary about us. *(Beat.)* I got invited to this midnight screening of *Psycho* at the Af. Am. House. People were gonna dress up, bring snacks. I should've totally gone. But all I want to do is hang out with you. That's all I really want to ever do.

CHARLOTTE: Same.

Pause. CHARLOTTE shakes her head from side to side. Something's upsetting her.

Something is happening to me and it's not going away.

JONNY sits up again, anxious.

JONNY: What is it?

CHARLOTTE: There's a girl. And I like her.

JONNY: OK.

CHARLOTTE: No, I mean I like her. I *like* her.

JONNY: And I mean ... "OK."

CHARLOTTE: I like her.

JONNY: Does she know?

CHARLOTTE: No. I mean, *I* didn't know. I mean, I knew I liked her but I didn't know I liked her in my *vagina*. And I've been reading a lot of feminist theory for this class I'm taking and I thought maybe it's the literature, because, you know, I agree.

JONNY: You told me in high school you were bi-sexual.

CHARLOTTE: I meant in theory. I said in theory we all are.

JONNY: I never thought it was theoretical.

CHARLOTTE holds JONNY's hand, plays with his fingers.

CHARLOTTE: This girl would sleep with me if she knew I liked her. She's *actually* gay.

JONNY: How do you know?

CHARLOTTE: She has a shaved head.

JONNY: *Her?*

CHARLOTTE: You know her?

JONNY: She's the only girl in the school with a shaved head.

CHARLOTTE: Claire.

JONNY: Right. Claire. *Claire?*

CHARLOTTE: I know. I don't understand it either. She's not cute.

JONNY: Well. She's ... butch.

CHARLOTTE: I do not understand how I can be attracted to her. It's gross.

JONNY: Do you think she's attracted to you?

CHARLOTTE: She smiled at me. *(Beat.)* She's so fucking brave with her shaved head. *(Beat.)* She asked me a question and she touched my arm. And when she did ...

JONNY: What?

CHARLOTTE: I felt this ... white light.

JONNY: You need to drink a lot more all the time because evidently you are repressing something that needs to happen.

CHARLOTTE: I love you so much. Thank you for listening to all of this.

JONNY: You don't need to be so freaked out.

CHARLOTTE: I don't even know *how* to have sex with a woman.

JONNY: *(A joke.)* There's a tremendous amount of information available on the internet.

CHARLOTTE: You know, I have her cell phone number.

JONNY: You have her *number?*

CHARLOTTE: She gave it to me. In case I wanted to study with her.

JONNY: She hit on you!

CHARLOTTE: She's totally recruiting me. *(Beat.)* Should I call her?

JONNY: This white light, Charlotte. You should explore this white light. We don't live in medieval times, Charlotte. You're not going to be hanged for a witch.

CHARLOTTE: Unless I move to Uganda.

JONNY: It's not a big deal.

CHARLOTTE: Two related observations. First, it is insane you saying it's not a big deal because you definitely think sex is a *very* big deal because you're still a virgin. So second, maybe you don't think it's a big deal because it's two women we're talking about and you don't count it as real sex. Which makes you a sexist, homophobic pig.

JONNY: OK. First, I am being reassuring to you because you are obviously stressed out and I don't think it is a big deal for you to have sex with Claire because you are *not* a virgin and therefore you don't have to worry about who to do it with for the first time. You chose for your first time to be with that weird wanna-be stand-up comic guy you went to Israel Camp with. I absolutely think lesbian sex is real sex, of course I do. I'm just saying ... don't freak out about it. It's OK.

Pause.

CHARLOTTE: Amy asked me if *you* were gay.

JONNY: Amy, who I dated freshman year?

CHARLOTTE: Uh huh, she didn't understand why you didn't sleep with her.

JONNY: Because she was gross.

CHARLOTTE: Then why did you go out with her?

JONNY: I didn't know she was gross until I started to go out with her. I told you. She kept potato chips under her bed in case she wanted to snack in the night. Her sheets were covered in crumbs. And she had very dry skin, it was medical, it was eczema, so you never even knew what was in the bed. Crumbs or flaked-off skin.

CHARLOTTE: But according to received wisdom, you're a young bundle of hormones, Jonny. You didn't want to explode into Amy? For the relief?

JONNY: *(An edge to his voice.)* Just because you want to sleep with a woman you don't get to do that gay thing when you assume everyone else is gay and not telling.

CHARLOTTE: I'm just asking. All the guys I know –

JONNY: Are assholes. It's probably why you want to sleep with Claire.

CHARLOTTE: *(Anxious.)* It's not because I'm gay?

JONNY: You're not gay, you're just cool. Look, I'm not like other guys. That's why you like me. And you're not like other girls. You're not like *anyone.* So yeah, it doesn't surprise me that you're bisexual. I have always been very uncool. Hence, still a virgin. I tried to have sex with Janelle but she was too Christian.

CHARLOTTE: You should date a nice Jew.

JONNY: Unfortunately, my favorite Jew is a lesbian.

CHARLOTTE: Bi-sexual. In theory, currently.

JONNY: I'm not going to graduate a virgin. That's too … like, I don't want to have to tell my son that. There's a girl. Monique. I have my eye on her.

CHARLOTTE: Great. You lose your heterosexual virginity to Monique. I'll lose my gay virginity to Claire. And we'll text each other in the middle to see how it's going.

JONNY: Deal.

Beat. CHARLOTTE stands decisively. Her world is unsteady for a moment.

You OK?

She turns on [or up?] some music.

CHARLOTTE: Let's dance!

She pulls JONNY to his feet.

I always feel self-conscious dancing. I'm sick of it! I'm sick of feeling self-conscious all the time. And it's just *you*, right? We've known each other for years. We've known each other for ten years!

JONNY: Twelve, and I don't want to dance.

CHARLOTTE: Look. Listen. I'm a terrible dancer. OK? But I'm going to do it and I'd like it if you'd join. This will be my first time, dancing unselfconsciously with another person in the room.

And with that, she begins to dance. She's not good. She's not bad. There's something painfully beautiful about her attempt to be free.

Dance!

JONNY joins in. There's some hand clapping, some finger snapping, no natural talent and it's sweet.

Why can some people just dance?

JONNY: Because they're shallow.

CHARLOTTE laughs.

CHARLOTTE: How bad do I look?

JONNY: Better than me. We have to turn this down, it's 3am.

He turns down [off?] the music.

Let me tell you something about racism. The world
expecting me to be able to dance just because I'm black.
That is racist. It's not an inherent ability. *(He stops dancing.)*
It's like in your dad's books. All the black people can
dance. Like ... there's a passage about all these black
people dancing at a club in New Orleans and it's totally
stereotypical. They're like ... rhythmically gyrating.

CHARLOTTE: I've seen black people rhythmically gyrate. Not
in this room, but ...

JONNY: You know why you're so scared of sleeping with
Claire?

CHARLOTTE: Because it's sexually deviant and also she has no
hair on her head, only under her arms?

JONNY: *(He stops dancing.)* Your father's fifth book, *Snow on
Peachtree Street,* don't you remember what it was about?

CHARLOTTE: Well knowing my dad's oeuvre as I do: someone
was murdered and Detective Grayson investigates and it's
not the first guy he talks to, it's not the second guy, it's not
the third guy, it's definitely the fourth guy, definitely the
fourth guy – oh no wait ... it was the second guy.

JONNY: Actually the plotting is more sophisticated than that
but ... *(Beat.)* He wrote about the tree. The big tree in your
yard. I remember hearing the description and thinking
hey, that's our tree. But instead of a tire hanging there was
a body hanging. And I thought maybe it was a lynching
because my mom said they lynched a man on that tree one
time. But it was a white girl hanging. Detective Grayson
thought she was a murder victim. But it was a red herring.
Because later it turned out she'd killed herself. Because she
was a lesbian.

CHARLOTTE: I haven't even read that one, so

JONNY: All I'm saying is, your dad is a little bit racist, and a
little bit homophobic.

CHARLOTTE: So is everyone's dad.

JONNY: How would I know?

CHARLOTTE: Tell me a secret, Jonny. You know all my secrets, now. I'm in love with a girl.

JONNY: In love?

CHARLOTTE: What if I'm not bi-sexual. What if I'm lesbian?

JONNY: Then … good. You can get fat and pretend it's a political statement. *(Beat.)* Call her. Take her out. I hear there's a Joan Baez Concert coming to town.

CHARLOTTE: Shall I do it right now?

JONNY: Go for it!

CHARLOTTE has her cell phone out.

CHARLOTTE: I feel like I'm about to jump off a cliff.

JONNY: You might not be into it. Four breasts may be two too many.

CHARLOTTE: *(Yelling.)* I want you to lose your virginity!

JONNY: I will. ASAP.

CHARLOTTE: I want you to lose it to me.

JONNY: But you're a lesbian.

CHARLOTTE: You love me.

JONNY: But I don't find you sexy.

CHARLOTTE: *(Angry.)* You always say it's like incest but it's *not*.

CHARLOTTE does something to her phone, then throws it across the room.

I erased her number. If this is a fucking phase, I'm going to let it pass without actually *doing* it. If I'm bi-sexual then I just want to be with men.

JONNY: OK. That's valid.

CHARLOTTE: Jonny, we have to do it sometime.

JONNY: Why do we? Because you've gotten really drunk?

CHARLOTTE: Because we're a man and a woman. We love each other. It's just inevitable. Doesn't it feel inevitable to you?

JONNY: It feels like an inevitable way to ruin the friendship.

CHARLOTTE: Why does it have to ruin anything? Let's just try it. And if we don't want to keep doing it together, with each other, then when we belong to other people, it'll be something they can't take away. But we might like it, Jonny. It might be amazing. We might get married and live happily ever after.

She undresses.

JONNY: It wouldn't work. I want to bring my kids up Christian. And ... black. You want to bring your kids up Jewish. We've talked about this.

CHARLOTTE: *(Talking over him.)* Oh look *beyond.* Let's get beyond fucking tribal thinking, can we? Please. Let's be the fucking future, Jonny. On a basic biological level, you must be attracted to me, right? I'm a twenty-one year old girl. I know I don't dress all sexy, but look. No clothes. This is prime meat. Everything sags starting next year. Capitalize now.

JONNY: You are very, very drunk right now. You're slurring.

That's not true. She is not slurring.

CHARLOTTE: *(Angry.)* You said you wanted to lose your virginity before the end of college. You're just scared. It's your defining fucking feature. You know how we go to the fair every year and you won't get on a single ride, you just watch me? Do you want that to be your whole fucking life? Climb on board!

JONNY: If I had sex with you right now it would be like date rape.

CHARLOTTE: *(Angry.)* Why won't you give us a chance? We love each other. We are *everything* to each other. When I'm with you the whole world can go fuck itself. That's what it feels like to be in real love! We're in love, Jonny. We should get fucking married and have babies and talk and touch and talk and touch and stop wasting time.

She walks or dances towards him, trying to be sexy. She comes over to him, kisses him.

Stop. Thinking.

She rushes away, rips off her underwear and lies on the bed.

OK. Now get over here and fuck me right now.

She lies on the bed and stares straight up at the ceiling, ready.

This is something we absolutely should do, Jonny. I know you're a virgin but I've never come with a guy before so I'm like a virgin in a way. Emotionally, I'm a virgin. I can come by myself and I've always been too embarrassed to show them how to do it but I could show you and I wouldn't be embarrassed because it's just you. And we could be good. And comfortable. Don't you want to be comfortable?

JONNY: I want so much more than that.

She looks over.

Painful moments as CHARLOTTE registers the rejection. Covers herself. JONNY can't bring himself to leave her like this, sits next to her, puts an arm around her.

SCENE THREE

Day. CHARLOTTE's family living room. Space. Money, taste, comfort, light. Off this room, exits to other implied locations in the large house. A sense of flow through the space.

JONNY stands alone in the middle of the room. Eventually, a grim HOWARD enters carrying a bucket. He barely acknowledges JONNY as he passes by, through and out to the kitchen. JONNY checks the time. He seems a little pissed.

LUCINDA enters.

LUCINDA: *(Hushed.)* Do you have a light, sugar?

JONNY: What?

LUCINDA: *(Louder.)* Do you have a light?

JONNY: I don't smoke.

LUCINDA: Must have been a fun night. Until she threw up all over the rose bushes. She's still sleeping it off.

JONNY: I'm here for Howard. And actually, I have to go soon. My mom's cooking a ham.

LUCINDA: I'm sure Howard will just be a few more minutes. He's just trying to rescue the roses. Because it's probably not good for them. Vomit.

JONNY: I don't know. They say manure …

LUCINDA: It's not the same. Because of acids.

JONNY: That makes sense.

HOWARD enters with the bucket. The bucket is now full of water.

HOWARD: *(To JONNY.)* I know you kids drink at your age. And I know it's spring break. But this is not OK.

He exits.

LUCINDA: If you want him in a better mood, compare him to Hitchcock again. He thinks it's the insight of the century. *(Beat.)* How's your head?

JONNY: Fine.

LUCINDA: I guess you guys were just out having fun and had a few too many.

JONNY: *(Non-committal.)* Yeah.

LUCINDA: She was pretty upset when she got home. Do you know what she was upset about?

JONNY: She was fine when we left her.

LUCINDA: You left her?

JONNY: She ran into other friends and stayed out.

LUCINDA: She's fragile, you know.

HOWARD return with the empty bucket.

HOWARD: *(To JONNY.)* I'm sorry I've kept you waiting. I just didn't expect you to be here on time. Charlotte's still sleeping it off.

LUCINDA: He wasn't with her.

HOWARD: What?

LUCINDA: *(Beat.)* Well, if anyone wants me I'll be in the sunroom.

LUCINDA exits.

HOWARD: I thought she was out with you.

JONNY: She was, but then a whole load of kids from high school showed up and Monique didn't want to stay and neither did I. Charlotte did. She was totally sober the last I saw her.

HOWARD: The thing is, Jonny, you're like a brother to her, right?

JONNY: Yeah.

HOWARD: So act like it. You don't leave a lady alone in a bar.

JONNY: *(Beat.)* You know, if we could get to this interview I'd appreciate it. My mom's cooking a ham and she's going to a lot of trouble.

HOWARD: Your mom's up and about, huh? That's got to feel good.

JONNY: It is Easter.

HOWARD: *(Astonished.)* Is it? Today?

JONNY: Yes.

HOWARD: Well, happy Easter!

JONNY: Anyway. *(Deep breath, ready to get down to business.)* Thank you for doing this.

HOWARD: Sure. Sure. You know, Jonny. She talked about you last night.

JONNY: She did?

HOWARD: Briefly. Want to know what she said?

JONNY: Not right now.

HOWARD: "I love him."

JONNY: Huh.

HOWARD: She mumbled it. She shouted it. Then she passed out.

JONNY: She said "him," right? She might not have meant me?

HOWARD: My daughter is in love with you.

JONNY: No, she isn't.

HOWARD: I can see what's in front of my face. It's no coincidence I write detective fiction. Ever since you started dating your new lady friend –

JONNY: Monique –

HOWARD: Charlotte has been off her food. Pale. Depressed. Won't talk to me, won't talk to Lula. But it's pretty obvious what the problem is.

JONNY: Charlotte and I are just friends.

HOWARD: *(Beat.)* You'd be lucky to have her.

JONNY: *(Beat.)* I'm not comfortable talking about her like this.

HOWARD: I met Monique. Let's talk man to man.

JONNY: I don't think we should.

HOWARD: Is she really the one? Or is it just that she has enormous breasts? And listen, I get that, good for you. That's fun. But are you responding to her *beyond* that? Because deep love, you know, that's about so much more. It's a spiritual connection. When that's not there there's nothing, you know?

JONNY: Monique and I have a spiritual connection, that's the whole –

HOWARD: Look, I know this is inappropriate. I just want to make sure that … I see between you and my daughter, I've seen … I've seen love. Real love. And I wanted to deny it. You're both so young. And she's my … she's my angel. But it's you. She's set her sights on you. And so I ask you, man to man, to consider if what you have with Monique is worth giving up the joy you could have with Charlotte for, who knows, the rest of your life.

Pause. JONNY tries to figure out how to address all this.

JONNY: It's not just about her breasts.

HOWARD: I see. Tell me.

JONNY: This is about family. I know you respect that. I am a Baptist.

HOWARD: *(Seeing the light.)* Aaaah …

JONNY: You don't want Charlotte marrying a Baptist and having little Christian babies, I know you don't want that.

HOWARD: Charlotte cannot be a Baptist. That is out of the question.

JONNY: She and I are not an option.

HOWARD: But at heart, we are all just people.

JONNY: I've got to get this interview done. It's half my grade.

HOWARD: Lucinda is not a Jew. Yes, she converted and I appreciate that, but she is not a Jew. At best, she is an extraordinarily lapsed Catholic. And although we define ourselves as Jews, our life is not very Jewish. You know that. I would *prefer* that Charlotte be with someone that defines themselves as a Jew. But above all, she must be happy. And if happiness to her is being with you, and if you're just worrying about your mother, then I implore you. Find a way. How long have I known you?

JONNY: Since I was nine.

HOWARD: This is the first time since you were nine-years-old that you have earned my respect. Your religion, your faith, your mother, those are concerns of substance. I admire them. Hey, more than that, I *get* it. I'm the same! My father's father was a rabbi! A *Polish* rabbi. Beard. Side curls. The whole nine yards. If he could have heard me talking this way it would have broken his heart. But fucking tribalism? I'm not for it. My wife. Lucinda. I turned, I saw her, I fucking *inhaled* her spirit and I was a dead man. God is love. You know that. And when I saw you with Monique it was clear, Jonny: there's no love there. There's no spark. There's just two black kids trying to do the right things by their parents. Life's too short for that shit. Know what I mean? What is that smell? Do you smell something?

JONNY: Yeah. Marijuana.

HOWARD: *(Baffled.)* Where's it coming from?

JONNY: *(Awkwardly.)* The sunroom?

Beat.

HOWARD: Excuse me.

HOWARD exits. CHARLOTTE is at the doorway that leads to upstairs.

CHARLOTTE: Am I dreaming or is someone getting high?

They look at each other for a few moments before:

JONNY: Your mom, I think.

CHARLOTTE: What are you doing here?

JONNY: My paper.

CHARLOTTE: I'm in a lot of pain.

JONNY: You know, your dad's going to be back in a second and there's already been a lot of distractions and I'd be grateful if you didn't suck out all of the energy in the room. If I don't have a paper I flunk.

CHARLOTTE: I feel so nauseous.

JONNY: You really hurt my feelings last night. And you embarrassed me.

CHARLOTTE: I'm sorry, I don't remember.

JONNY: You don't remember anything?

CHARLOTTE: I remember a lot of shouting. I remember I was crying and you left me. Downtown. Did you leave me downtown? On the street?

JONNY: Yes.

JONNY is trying to decide whether or not to give in when LUCINDA and HOWARD enter.

LUCINDA: I have to smoke something, Howard. I need a fucking crutch, alright. I need one.

HOWARD: I bought you an electronic cigarette!

LUCINDA: You're like a spy, you know that? Following me around, checking up on me.

HOWARD: It was supposed to be a secret? That stuff stinks. Where'd you get it?

LUCINDA: *(Exaggerated Southern accent.)* I went down to the docks, Detective Grayson. I sold myself to a young man in blue. While he was sleeping, I stole his marijuana. Don't arrest me, please God don't arrest me, I'll do anything! Anything!

Beat.

HOWARD: What is that?

LUCINDA: That was supposed to be: stop *badgering* me.

HOWARD: Is that supposed to be funny?

LUCINDA: Uh huh, exactly. It was a joke.

HOWARD: A joke, like a parody of my work?

LUCINDA: You put the work out there, the public will judge it.

HOWARD: You're not the *public*. You're my wife.

JONNY: I'm here.

HOWARD: Yes we know you're here.

JONNY: Oh.

CHARLOTTE: Did I wake you guys last night?

LUCINDA: How are you feeling, honey?

CHARLOTTE: How do I look?

LUCINDA: I'll get you some aspirin.

LUCINDA exits.

HOWARD: You absolutely woke us last night.

CHARLOTTE: Let's talk about it later. I'll go to the kitchen. I don't want to suck all of the air out of the room. I know you men have important business.

HOWARD: You scared me.

CHARLOTTE: I'm sorry.

HOWARD: That was too drunk. If you have a problem –

CHARLOTTE: I don't.

HOWARD: A drinking problem or a problem that's making you drink, you come to me. We talk about it.

CHARLOTTE: OK.

HOWARD: I'm your Dad. There's no problem I won't help you fix.

JONNY: Howard, we really need to –

HOWARD: One second, please Jonny. *(To CHARLOTTE.)* If you came home and said I murdered someone. I would say, "Where's the corpse?" Then I'd cut it in tiny pieces and feed it to barnyard animals. And if by some miracle the police found you anyway, I'd say I did it.

CHARLOTTE: I think the better parenting choice would be to make me take responsibility for the crime.

HOWARD: I'd never let you get the chair.

CHARLOTTE: I'm in love with a woman.

Pause.

HOWARD: Jonny, I'm going to have to ask you to come back.

JONNY: Right.

HOWARD: We'll find another time.

JONNY: Sure. Great.

LUCINDA enters and hands a glass and aspirin to CHARLOTTE: JONNY starts to exit.

CHARLOTTE: *(Weakly.)* Can you stay, Jonny?

JONNY has no intention of staying. He gets his things together.

LUCINDA: *(Brightly.)* Did you get what you need, honey?

JONNY ignores her, exits. CHARLOTTE washes down the aspirin. Chokes.

CHARLOTTE: Is this vodka?

LUCINDA: Hair of the dog, sugar-pie.

HOWARD: Are you fucking serious?

HOWARD snatches the glass away from CHARLOTTE.

LUCINDA: It works. I'm trying to help.

HOWARD: Then be a mother. Your daughter has something to tell you.

CHARLOTTE: No, I don't.

HOWARD: Yes, you do.

CHARLOTTE: I don't. I shouldn't have said anything. It doesn't matter. This isn't something we need to have a family summit about.

HOWARD: I think it is.

CHARLOTTE: Why?

HOWARD: Because ... I don't know. Because it sounds like something we should have a conversation about.
(To LUCINDA.) She's not in love with Jonny. She's in love with ...

CHARLOTTE: Claire.

LUCINDA: *(Intrigued.)* Who's he?

HOWARD: A woman.

LUCINDA: *(Fascinated.)* Really?

LUCINDA produces a half-smoked joint from her pocket, lights up.

HOWARD: Really?

LUCINDA: Really.

CHARLOTTE: Since when do you smoke pot?

LUCINDA: Since I quit nicotine for your father.

HOWARD: It stinks.

LUCINDA: You used to love smoking pot.

HOWARD: We're talking about Charlotte.

LUCINDA: Honey, she's in college. Everyone experiments, in college. That's what you were, at first. My Jewish experiment. *(To CHARLOTTE.)* I've slept with a woman.

HOWARD: Oh Jesus.

CHARLOTTE: *(Shocked, to HOWARD.)* Did you know that?

LUCINDA: Honey, he was there.

CHARLOTTE: This is isn't like that. This isn't that.

HOWARD: *(To CHARLOTTE.)* I just like clarity, OK? Just so I understand what we're talking about here. Are you gay?

CHARLOTTE: I don't know. Probably not. Maybe. I don't know. I'm in love with someone named Claire. And it's been going on for a while. And it turns out that when you're in love you want to tell everybody. But I felt like I shouldn't, I kept thinking we'd break up and nobody needs to know it ever happened, but we keep not breaking up, we're really in love and so now I have to tell you guys. Because I love you. I'm so sorry. I know this is not what you want for me.

HOWARD: *(Quickly.)* We don't care. *(To LUCINDA.)* Do you care? *(To CHARLOTTE.)* I don't care.

179

LUCINDA: If you were gay, that's fine. But you are not a lesbian. I promise you.

CHARLOTTE: How do you know?

LUCINDA: You're just *not*. Remember all through high school you had a crush on Mr. Conner. You were obsessed with him. And there was that boy, that boy you liked. Edward. Little gay girls have crushes on girls, honey.

CHARLOTTE: Yeah.

LUCINDA: You're just a free spirit and your father and I love that about you.

HOWARD: You know about twenty years ago I was in the West Village in Manhattan eating a popsicle and this guy with very short shorts, beautiful young man, bare-chested, smiled at me from across the street and he called out, "Can I have a suck on your popsicle?" And I knew what he meant.

LUCINDA: No kidding.

HOWARD: I have always wished that I had the courage to experiment. Like a real artist. *(To CHARLOTTE.)* I'm very proud of you.

CHARLOTTE: I want you to meet Claire. Can I bring her home for a weekend?

LUCINDA and HOWARD exchange quick glances.

LUCINDA: Well of course, honey.

HOWARD: Great. Can't wait to meet Claire.

LUCINDA: Do you have a picture?

CHARLOTTE: Do you really want to see a picture?

LUCINDA: Yes!

CHARLOTTE goes over to a laptop and logs into her Facebook page.

CHARLOTTE: She's not, I guess, super cute in the conventional sense. But she's very smart. And Dad, she's half-Jewish.

HOWARD: Well, hooray.

CHARLOTTE shows them the picture.

CHARLOTTE: Here.

HOWARD and LUCINDA take in the photograph.

LUCINDA: Now *she* is a lesbian.

CHARLOTTE: You see? That's not nice. You say it like an insult.

LUCINDA: No, I just mean she is definitely … her mother would not be able to reassure her that –

CHARLOTTE: Who says I want reassurance?

Beat.

HOWARD: Honey, however you want to be. Whoever you want to be with. We love you.

LUCINDA: Although if you're going to be with a woman, why would you want to be with a woman who looks like a man? I don't get it.

CHARLOTTE: I don't get it either. But I can't stop.

Beat.

LUCINDA: Do you want to stop?

CHARLOTTE: Yes.

LUCINDA: Why?

CHARLOTTE: BECAUSE SHE'S NOT WHO I AM!

CHARLOTTE runs up the stairs. Pause. LUCINDA takes a hit off the joint.

HOWARD: Huh.

LUCINDA: While things are in pieces, I'm seeing someone.

HOWARD freezes. Pause.

HOWARD: Whatever we say next we will say quietly and carefully. I will not have her more upset.

LUCINDA: She's not a kid any more, Howard.

HOWARD: She's my kid. *(Beat.)* You remember those wrists? Those skinny white bug-bitten nine-year-old arms and those wrists. And the promises we made.

LUCINDA: I'm sorry. But she's all grown up.

HOWARD takes difficult breaths.

HOWARD: Jesus, what is happening?

SCENE FOUR

Still the living room. Late. Dark. CHARLOTTE and JONNY. JONNY is cold.

CHARLOTTE: How was Easter?

JONNY: I can't just hang out.

CHARLOTTE: I know.

JONNY: I've got company.

CHARLOTTE: I get it. *(Beat.)* I said bring Monique.

JONNY: Monique doesn't want to see you.

CHARLOTTE: Wow.

JONNY: You were a total asshole. To her. To me.

CHARLOTTE: You have to get over it.

JONNY: It was less than twenty-four hours ago, so I don't think I have to get over it right now.

CHARLOTTE: I need you to get over it by the time we get back to school. I was drunk.

JONNY: So? *In vino veritas*. Ever hear that saying?

CHARLOTTE: Everyone's heard that saying.

JONNY: How much do you remember of what you said?

CHARLOTTE: You know what I remember? I was upset and I needed you to be there for me.

JONNY: You have a problem with selfishness.

CHARLOTTE: Jonny? Don't break up with me.

JONNY: We're not together.

CHARLOTTE: Yes we are.

JONNY: Here's what I'm starting to think. You have real psychological problems.

CHARLOTTE: Obviously I do. I tried to kill myself when I was nine.

JONNY: But I mean now. You have real problems now.

CHARLOTTE: So?

JONNY: So they're becoming unmanageable. For me.

CHARLOTTE: Oh my God.

JONNY: Look it's not my job to …

CHARLOTTE: To what?

JONNY: You make being your friend a job.

CHARLOTTE: Oh.

JONNY: I'm just being honest.

CHARLOTTE: Well good because honesty is key.

JONNY: All I do is pick you up. And before, I had no one else. Now I do. I have someone. And how do you think it makes her feel, if I'm running around after you all the time?

CHARLOTTE: Jealous?

JONNY: No, not jealous. It disgusts her. It makes her feel like a girl that's not my girlfriend is running my life.

CHARLOTTE: That's what she says?

JONNY: Yes.

CHARLOTTE: And you *let* her say that? You didn't stand up for us? You know that *I* am seeing someone – I would never let Claire come between us. I don't think who you fuck is more important than your best friend.

JONNY: Well I'm not *fucking* Monique so there's that. Because we're looking for something a little deeper. *We* are looking to be best friends. Because that's what a relationship is. So I know you and Claire never stop fucking, and I know it's the most incredible thing that's ever happened to you and I am happy for you, I really am. But it is time to accept that our road has divided. Different journeys. Different destinations. For sure.

CHARLOTTE: I'm off on the road less travelled all by myself, huh?

JONNY: You don't even like me. Did you know that? You told me last night.

CHARLOTTE: Because *I'm* jealous. I'm jealous of Monique. You have to let people behave badly sometimes.

JONNY: You have a drinking problem. And by the way so does Claire.

CHARLOTTE: Thank you for telling me that. That's what friends do.

JONNY: Monique can't believe I'm over here tonight. Neither can my mom.

CHARLOTTE: Your mom knows we had a fight?

JONNY: We didn't have a fight, Charlotte. You screamed at me in the street like a drunken maniac for fifteen minutes. And I tried to calm you down and put you in a cab and you tried to make out with me. In front of my girlfriend. And when I pushed you off, which was the only way to get you off, you tried to call the cops. And then you told Monique I was gay. Because I wouldn't fuck you that time. Because I don't fuck her. And you said it was extra proof that I was gay that I wouldn't fuck her because she has such enormous breasts. And she explained to you, as I have done like a thousand times, that we don't fuck because we're Christians. And you told her the two of you, just her and you, should go off and find another bar and really talk about that because you found it impossible to believe that any intelligent person truly believed in the risen Christ.

Pause.

CHARLOTTE: Huh.

JONNY: And I think you meant all that.

CHARLOTTE: Jonny, she really does have enormous breasts.

JONNY: That's one of the things I like about her. When we are married, I will engage with them more fully.

CHARLOTTE: You are *not* getting married.

JONNY: I think that we will.

CHARLOTTE: That's ridiculous.

JONNY: See! You meant every word you said so how can we be friends?

CHARLOTTE: I don't think you're gay. I'm sorry.

JONNY: You're sorry you're gay and you're taking it out on everyone else.

CHARLOTTE: Do you really think I'm gay?

JONNY: I can't talk about this any more. I can't. Ever! I can't give it a single second of my time. I'm really happy you told your parents. I told you they'd be cool. I have to go.

CHARLOTTE: Can I see your mom before school starts up?

JONNY: Why?

CHARLOTTE: To say good-bye.

JONNY: Not while Monique's there.

CHARLOTTE: But school starts Tuesday. *(Beat.)* You shouldn't have told her about last night. Gossip's a sin.

JONNY: You know what my mom said? She said, "That child's always been troubled." She's praying for *you*, Charlotte. While churches across the nation are praying for her.

CHARLOTTE: Prayer doesn't do any good, Jonny. Magic doesn't exist. Grow up!

Silence.

We're over, aren't we?

JONNY: Fucking done.

He exits.

CHARLOTTE: Jonny!

Loud, loud music. A woman's voice. Religious. Etta James' 'At Last',* maybe. But soaring.

CHARLOTTE runs after JONNY: We fluidly transition into:

* See Music Use Note on Copyright Page

SCENE FIVE

Outside. Moonlight. A huge tree. An ancient thick rope hanging from a branch, a tire at the end.

JONNY is waiting under the tree. He's in a dark suit. He's in despair.

CHARLOTTE comes out. She's barefoot, in a loose, cotton nightgown. Cautious. They stare at each other for a few moments.

JONNY makes a gesture that says "Here I am." A sort of helpless shrug.

CHARLOTTE: I'm so sorry for your loss.

> *Pause.*

Have you cried?

> *JONNY shakes his head.*

You should cry a lot. As she's dead. You didn't cry at the funeral.

JONNY: And you weren't invited.

CHARLOTTE: That's why I sat at the back.

> *Beat.*

JONNY: I was happy you were there.

> *Beat.*

CHARLOTTE: I kept looking at you. You never looked back.

> *Beat.*

JONNY: So you know I'm engaged?

CHARLOTTE: Yes. Congratulations. I hope you'll be very happy. Really.

JONNY: I can't get married.

CHARLOTTE: Why not?

JONNY: Because I did something bad.

Beat.

CHARLOTTE: What did you do?

JONNY: I had sex with a guy that I hate who's really into comic books.

CHARLOTTE: What?

JONNY: I had sex with a guy that I hate who's really into comic books.

CHARLOTTE: Huh.

Beat.

JONNY: Actually that is an ongoing situation.

CHARLOTTE: *(Beat, then slowly.)* You're having sex with a guy you hate who's really into comic books. *(Beat.)* As of when?

JONNY: His name is Jonah.

CHARLOTTE: Jonah.

JONNY: He's awful. *(Beat.)* I don't know what to do. I can't stop. He lives in a shit hole, there are roaches and a ton of musty, vintage Aquamans. I can't get married. I have no idea what I'm doing. Monique is wondering where I am right now. You have to help me. I don't want to be doing what I'm doing. I don't want to be ... *(Can't find the end of the sentence.)* I kind of don't want to be.

CHARLOTTE: *(Hesitant.)* It's OK. You're OK. *(Beat.)* So ... I'm a little confused.

JONNY: Yeah me too.

CHARLOTTE: Is Jonah your first ... Gentleman Caller?

Pause.

Jonny?

JONNY: I can't believe my mom's dead. I can't call her on the phone. I can't write her a letter. She's just gone. And all through the funeral I should have been thinking of her. But I wasn't. I was thinking of Edward. *(Beat.)* From camp?

CHARLOTTE: Edward from camp who was pretty like a girl?

Beat.

JONNY: Edward who was pretty like a girl.

CHARLOTTE: He was first?

JONNY nods.

When we were eleven? *(Beat.)* You knew when we were eleven?

JONNY: No! I didn't know anything! We shouldn't talk about this.

CHARLOTTE: I think you want to talk. I think that's why you're loitering in my yard.

Pause.

JONNY: My mom's in a box, I wish it was me. I'm going to hell, you know that?

CHARLOTTE: There's no such thing as hell, you know that?

Beat.

JONNY: It was Edward's idea. And I don't know why. I don't know why he looked at me and was like – yeah. You. What did he see?

CHARLOTTE: He saw you, Jonny. You're lovely.

Pause.

Why didn't you tell me?

JONNY: It happened one time. Just one time. And I never thought about it. I think I repressed the memory. That's why I didn't tell you. It was like … It was like ear wax, you know?

Ear wax that's in so deep you forget it's there, even though it's making everything fuzzy. *(Angry.)* It fucked me up.

Pause as CHARLOTTE processes.

CHARLOTTE: So Edward happened. Then repression?

JONNY: Yes.

CHARLOTTE: Then Jonah.

JONNY: Yeah, pretty much.

CHARLOTTE: Pretty much? *(Beat, heart racing, regarding whiskey.)* Did you drink all of this?

JONNY: Yeah, I'm wasted.

Pause. JONNY hiccups.

CHARLOTTE: Pretty much? *(Scared of the answer.)* Have you been with guys this whole time, Jonny?

JONNY: I have *not* been with men this whole time. I've been with Monique. And before that Janelle. And before that Amy.

CHARLOTTE: A string of good Christian women. One with Eczema.

Pause.

JONNY: I didn't tell you because I didn't want it to be true. When you say things out loud they become true. I say almost nothing to Jonah. And he only talks about comics. *(Beat.)* I've been very fucking lonely, Charlotte.

Beat. CHARLOTTE controls her temper. Takes charge.

CHARLOTTE: Well you've said it out loud and it sounds true so you have to tell Monique.

JONNY: Tell her what?

CHARLOTTE: That you're *gay.* Jesus, poor Monique.

JONNY: *(Furious.)* Since when do you give a *shit* about Monique?

Pause. JONNY hiccups.

And I'm not necessarily *gay*. Because it's not *real* if it's because someone else fucking fucked me up. I just need to get better.

CHARLOTTE: Oh Jonny.

Somehow they're together now and she might be holding him.

JONNY: I really didn't know.

CHARLOTTE: So you've experienced the white light.

JONNY: Oh yes. Many times now. *(Beat.)* I heard you and Claire broke up, by the way. I'm sorry.

CHARLOTTE: Yes, it was terrible. I called you a couple of times, you never picked up. *(Beat, hard.)* I missed you. This has been very hard.

JONNY: For me too.

Beat.

CHARLOTTE: Claire's with men, now. She grew her hair back.

Beat. JONNY registers this. Fascinating.

JONNY: No way.

CHARLOTTE: Yup. She was a total LUG. Lesbian Until Graduation.

He hiccups again.

JONNY: Fuck these hurt. They really hurt.

CHARLOTTE: I'm going to give you a shock OK? That will get rid of them.

JONNY: OK.

They stare at each other. She punches him in the stomach. So hard. He doubles up. She stands over him. He hiccups.

ACT TWO

SCENE ONE

Five years later. Spring.

CHARLOTTE and JONNY at a wooden picnic table under the tree in the backyard. The table is set for lunch. Plates. Wine. The swing has gone.

JONNY: I am *really* into the idea.

CHARLOTTE: *(Thrilled.)* You are?

JONNY: I'd love it.

CHARLOTTE: We don't know if we're looking for a donor or a father or something in between but we definitely want kids.

JONNY: You've always wanted kids.

CHARLOTTE: And so has she. I mean this is way down the line, she has to finish her residency so it's way too early to bring it up with you but I just wanted to tell you because Martha and I talk about it all the time, which means we talk about you, and would you, or wouldn't you.

JONNY: It makes sense. We always talked about what great parents we'd make.

CHARLOTTE: And Martha, obviously. I mean she and I would be the parents. And you'd be – I don't know. We would have to discuss it.

JONNY: We'll figure out our own rules.

CHARLOTTE: Yes we will. I should mention that Martha also has a very close friend who's a gay man and she's interested in talking to him too but I think he wants kids with his partner.

JONNY: *(Disconcerted.)* I guess this is all a long way off. We'll figure it out.

(LUCINDA enters from the house carrying a huge bowl of salad.)

LUCINDA: Hey ya'll!

CHARLOTTE: *(To JONNY.)* But I am very psyched that you're into the idea and I will tell Martha.

LUCINDA: *(Sitting down.)* Jesus, Jonny, you look great. You've … filled out. I don't know. Something.

JONNY: I swim a lot.

LUCINDA: In the ocean?

JONNY: The ocean. The gym.

CHARLOTTE: He looks great, doesn't he?

HOWARD enters from the house with four glasses.

HOWARD: How's everybody?

CHARLOTTE: Can I do anything?

HOWARD: No, I think we're all squared away. Let's eat.

HOWARD sits. JONNY serves himself some salad.

CHARLOTTE: I really think we can do the wedding back here.

HOWARD: The front yard's much bigger.

CHARLOTTE: I would rather invite fewer people, and do it back here. It's so romantic under the tree.

JONNY: Where's the tire swing?

CHARLOTTE: I took it down to see how it would look with just a chuppah back here.

HOWARD: The invitations have already been sent.

JONNY: It's better out front. The lawn is flatter. You can set up a dance floor more easily. Are we doing dancing?

CHARLOTTE: Oh yes. Dinner. Dancing. Unfortunately for me, Martha loves dancing.

LUCINDA: She's very good.

JONNY: Charlotte, you're going to have to tell me my best man duties. I mean, traditionally it would be for me to get you drunk and take you to a strip club. But you've stopped drinking.

CHARLOTTE: That doesn't mean I can't go to a strip club.

HOWARD: No one's going to a strip club. *(Beat.)* In my opinion. I mean, of course it's none of my business.

CHARLOTTE: Don't you want to come, Dad? Don't the dads come?

LUCINDA: I'm coming.

HOWARD: I think strip clubs degrade women. So I don't want to go. And I'm surprised you'd participate in something like that, Charlotte.

JONNY: I was actually joking. I can't think of anything worse than going to a strip club. Unless it was full of men. *(A slightly weird moment.)* We can do whatever you want.

LUCINDA: Will you be bringing a date to the wedding, Jonny?

CHARLOTTE: No, he won't.

JONNY: Excuse me?

CHARLOTTE: Jonny specializes in the three-second relationship. I don't want some dude he just met competing for attention at my wedding.

LUCINDA: Making up for lost time, huh, Jonny? Good for you.

JONNY: *(Touched.)* Thanks. *(Beat.)* I love the strawberries in the salad.

CHARLOTTE: Is there something apart from wine to pour into these glasses?

LUCINDA: Howard, where's the lemonade? I made lemonade.

HOWARD: Oh.

LUCINDA: Well, go get it.

HOWARD: Shit.

CHARLOTTE: I'll go.

LUCINDA: No you just got off a plane. Howard, go get it.

HOWARD: Anything for anybody else?

JONNY: Just the lemonade would be great.

> *A split second of tension between HOWARD and JONNY. No one else notices. HOWARD trudges back to the house.*

> Actually I met a guy I like a couple of weeks ago. His name is Will. He's an airline pilot. Seriously, he's an airline pilot.

LUCINDA: Where'd you meet him?

JONNY: Church.

> *The slightest of pauses.*

CHARLOTTE: Well if you're still seeing him in three months. Maybe. As long as he doesn't distract you from your best man duties.

JONNY: You got the ceremony all figured out?

CHARLOTTE: We found a very accommodating lady rabbi. Dad did.

JONNY: That's great.

CHARLOTTE: But I need you to help me find a dress. Or pants? Do you think I should wear pants? Like a tux?

LUCINDA: Honey, you're not wearing a tux.

JONNY: A tux might be amazing.

LUCINDA: She's gay, she's not a man.

JONNY: *(To LUCINDA.)* What happened to your wedding dress?

LUCINDA: eBay.

CHARLOTTE: I'm bringing options home tomorrow afternoon. Everyone has to give their opinion.

JONNY: What's the guest list up to?

CHARLOTTE: Eighty.

HOWARD returns with a pitcher of lemonade.

HOWARD: Did you tell Jonny the big news?

CHARLOTTE: I didn't know there was big news.

HOWARD: My dad's flying in from New York!

JONNY: That's great.

HOWARD: He's delighted about the whole thing!

LUCINDA: Bullshit.

HOWARD: Seriously. I was terrified to tell him. I really thought it might be the end of our relationship altogether. But he was so good about it. He actually said "*mazel tov*" which is more than he said when I told him I was marrying Lucinda. And he explained, and this is very interesting, that the Torah says *nothing* about two women. So Halachically speaking, it's fine!

CHARLOTTE: *(To JONNY.)* Isn't that nice? I'm invisible.

JONNY: That beats visible and stoned to death.

HOWARD: Who's stoning you to death?

JONNY: You don't think gay men are oppressed?

HOWARD: Not by the Jews. We *get* being oppressed. So we try not to do it to other people.

JONNY: Tell it to Palestine.

HOWARD: Watch it!

LUCINDA: My Daddy had a rule. No politics at the table.

HOWARD: Otherwise known as the "if you don't agree with me, you may not speak" rule.

LUCINDA: Otherwise known as being polite.

CHARLOTTE: Can you two not bicker?

Beat.

LUCINDA: I also reached out to my remaining family. They told me to go fuck myself.

CHARLOTTE: I didn't know that. *(Beat.)* That's nice that you reached out though.

LUCINDA: Fuck them.

HOWARD: *(To JONNY.)* You know Martha's Jewish?

JONNY: I did know that.

LUCINDA: She is whip smart. And very pretty. Can't wait to have her in the family. A surgeon! I really get off on telling people that. I say, "My daughter's getting married to another woman." And just as they get that pitying look in their eye I say, "She's a brain surgeon," and it just blows their mind.

CHARLOTTE: She's not a brain surgeon, mom.

LUCINDA: Doesn't matter.

LUCINDA lights a cigarette.

HOWARD: Seriously? At lunch? At the table?

LUCINDA: You betcha. Over strawberries.

Beat.

JONNY: It feels so good to be eating a meal with y'all. I can't believe how long it's been.

CHARLOTTE: Jonny and I haven't seen each other for almost a year. Except on Skype. But it's not the same as in the flesh.

She kisses JONNY on the cheek, squeezes his arm, something.

HOWARD: So what's going on with your mom's house, Jonny?

JONNY: We're closing tomorrow.

HOWARD: Nice people, my new neighbors?

JONNY: I think so. Husband. Wife. Couple of kids.

LUCINDA: End of an era, huh?

JONNY: Especially for my family. That house belonged to my great, great, great grandfather. But it's been five years since my mom passed and I never come back here so ... I cut the cord. *(Beat.)* I really love California.

CHARLOTTE: Jonny and I have a plan. We'll come back here, once a year –

HOWARD: More than that I hope.

CHARLOTTE: Once a year together, no partners, no spouses, just us. At the fair.

JONNY: I'll watch her ride the rollercoaster.

Pause.

HOWARD: *(To JONNY.)* So how's the teaching going?

JONNY: I'm taking a break, actually. I've been working on a book this past year, and with the sale of the house and the advance I got –

HOWARD: Advance on the house?

JONNY: Advance on the book.

HOWARD: It's being published? *(Beat.)* That's great. What is it? Something academic?

JONNY: No, I guess it's fiction.

HOWARD: *(Disconcerted.)* Really?

JONNY: Yes.

CHARLOTTE: It's called *Letters I Never Wrote My Mother* and it's beautiful.

JONNY: It's kind of a memoir.

HOWARD: Which is it? Fiction or memoir? They're extremely different.

JONNY: Well … it's like … it's what I *wish* had happened. I don't know. It's kind of a new genre. Maybe.

HOWARD: Oh.

LUCINDA: They gave you an advance? People must be pretty excited about it.

CHARLOTTE: He get's all tense talking about it. If you want to know any more, Google him. Or wait until he does all the morning talk shows.

JONNY: It's not going to be big like that.

CHARLOTTE: It might be. They think it might be.

LUCINDA: How's your new one coming, Howard? People excited about it?

HOWARD: Fuck you.

CHARLOTTE: Guys!

HOWARD: People are excited about it. I also got an advance. Carol and I are talking about taking a trip with it. Around the world.

LUCINDA: You hate to travel.

HOWARD: Not with her.

CHARLOTTE: You promised we could eat together as a family and be civil.

Pause. LUCINDA does her hypnosis inhalation thing.

JONNY: You do that *and* smoke?

LUCINDA: And drink.

She takes a sip of wine.

HOWARD: Carol's coming to the wedding. Charlotte said it was OK.

CHARLOTTE: *(To LUCINDA.)* I was going to discuss it with you.

No response from LUCINDA.

JONNY: Thanks for letting me stay at the house tonight.

LUCINDA: You're welcome.

HOWARD: *(At the same time.)* You're welcome. *(To LUCINDA.)* Not your house anymore.

CHARLOTTE: I'm so frightened you guys are going to ruin the wedding.

LUCINDA: *(To CHARLOTTE.)* I am so tired of being your Mammie. "Everything's alright chil', don't you worry about me not having my freedom now, sleep on my titties, I'll sing you a lullaby?"

JONNY: *(Not offended, awed.)* Jesus.

LUCINDA: *(To CHARLOTTE.)* Honey, I can't perform for you any more. Especially now I'm off my meds.

CHARLOTTE: I don't want you to perform for me.

LUCINDA: Yes you do, but I'm done.

HOWARD: You shouldn't *be* off your meds. What kind of therapist are you seeing?

LUCINDA: One who explained I wasn't unhappy because I had a chemical imbalance. I was unhappy because I was married to you!

HOWARD: *(Violently.)* Behave! She's getting married and you will behave! You want to hate me, you want to blame me –

LUCINDA: He plays the victim. But the truth is he fell out of love with me years ago and was too chicken to admit it.

HOWARD: I would have toughed it out.

LUCINDA: There is nothing successful about an unhappy marriage, you idiot.

HOWARD: There is! Kept promises and character and loyalty –

LUCINDA: You are happier because I left! You are happier with this mouse Carol because I left!

HOWARD: That is not true.

LUCINDA: Do you fuck her?

JONNY and CHARLOTTE make a silent joint decision to leave. They get up.

He wouldn't fuck me! You two know how important sex is! Well he stopped making love to me!

HOWARD: Behave.

LUCINDA: It was perfunctory! It was the service given by the teenager at the gas tank. Quick and jabby. A summer job he had to do. Howard we are approaching old age! I intend to enjoy my twilight making love!

HOWARD: Can't you keep your emotions in check long enough for us all to have lunch? She's in from D.C. once every six months. Can you not make it so that she never wants to come home? Please?

HOWARD grabs some plates and heads back to the house, containing his emotions. Beat. CHARLOTTE runs after him.

LUCINDA: Sorry about that, Jonny.

JONNY: I've been in therapy too, over the last few years. It's life-changing, huh?

LUCINDA: Literally.

JONNY: I'm sorry this is happening to you, Lula.

LUCINDA takes his hand across the table.

LUCINDA: Jonny. This whole gay marriage thing is very exciting and God bless. But you want my advice? Don't do it.

LUCINDA studies JONNY's hand.

JONNY: You reading my fortune?

LUCINDA: My Daddy was a real asshole but he was so great when I was a little girl and I didn't know he was an asshole, you know? I'd rub the knuckles of his right hand while he was driving. And we'd play Hank Williams because I was the only one of my sisters that liked Hank Williams and he loved me for it. Honestly, I don't know if I really liked Hank Williams or if I just wanted him to love me a little bit more than my sisters. Sometimes I think I was testing his love when I introduced him to Howard. I knew he'd hate him, I knew it. But I wanted unconditional love, you know. Not from Howard. From my dad. And when I saw I didn't have it ... when he made threats about disinheriting me, marrying a kike ... that sent me right down the aisle.

JONNY: *(Gently.)* You got a beautiful daughter out of it.

LUCINDA: But she's always been a Daddy's girl.

JONNY: Supply and demand. He was always holed up writing.

LUCINDA: Will you do me a favor, Jonny? Dance with me at her wedding? There's nothing worse than being at a wedding and having no one to dance with.

JONNY: Fine. But stand forewarned. I am a terrible dancer.

LUCINDA: We'll just do the slow ones. They're easy. Just got to hold me and sway.

SCENE TWO

The family living room, the next afternoon. HOWARD, very agitated, is reading something on his laptop.

HOWARD: *(Yelling.)* Jonny! Jonny get down here!

Furious, he paces until JONNY enters.

JONNY: What's up?

HOWARD: *(Pointing at the computer.)* What is that? What the fuck is that?

JONNY: Your laptop.

HOWARD: What's *on* the laptop.

JONNY goes over to the laptop and starts reading. He's flustered.

JONNY: I don't know how this got here.

HOWARD: Is that the problem? Or is the problem that it *exists?*

JONNY: How did you even find it?

HOWARD: I Googled your name to find out about your fucking book deal.

JONNY: This is something I wrote a very long time ago. I didn't even know it was online. I apologize.

HOWARD: I only read the first paragraph.

JONNY: Good.

HOWARD: Now they want a credit card number. Why should I pay? You're right here in my house. You can tell me face to face why, as you state in your first paragraph, my novels are case studies of casual sexism, racism and homophobia?

Pause.

JONNY: I was going to interview you.

HOWARD: Oh yes! Truffaut. Hitchcock. That was a lot of smoke you blew up my ass.

JONNY: You weren't available. Remember?

HOWARD: So you libeled me? Does Charlotte know about this?

JONNY: No.

HOWARD Googles something on the laptop.

It was just a paper. My professor sent it to the world's most obscure journal.

HOWARD: Great! You Google *my* name and this comes up!

JONNY: Sorry.

HOWARD: How the fuck have I offended you? What did I ever do except write books and love my beautiful gay daughter? Except believe she could be the first female president because there should be a woman president. I have *always* thought women are better than men! And by the way, I have always loved homosexuals! My agent is a homosexual! Without homosexuals the world would be less beautiful! I know that, I get that, I'm one of the good guys! You have offended me. Very, very intensely offended me. That's personal. Now let's get legal. This is slander. I want it off the internet.

JONNY: That's fine, that's great, I told you, it was never meant to be published. I just wrote it really fast, my professor thought it was really good …

HOWARD: I give a lot of money to that school, what professor, what's his name?

JONNY: It was a she.

HOWARD: Of course it was.

JONNY: *(Cold.)* She was black too. Does that make her even more suspect?

Beat.

HOWARD: You think I'm a racist?

JONNY: It's not slander.

HOWARD: So you stand by this?

JONNY: It's a critical analysis. Authors attract critics. That's legitimate.

HOWARD: Fine. Justify your position. Clarify your position.

JONNY: It is *very* clear on the page. In your twenty-nine books there are forty-two homosexual characters. Thirty-eight are what I call underworld figures. Of the shadows and the streets. Criminal.

HOWARD: It's detective fiction, Jonny. Lots of criminals in it.

JONNY: You objectify women constantly. The first sentence in your ninth book is "her seventeen-year-old breasts looked like miniature upside down pie crusts before they'd been baked."

HOWARD: Should I not describe breasts? Is it sexist to acknowledge that breasts exist and to ninety percent of the male population they are phenomenal!

JONNY: Of the one hundred and eight victims in your novels eighty-three are women.

HOWARD: You can't interpret literature with math.

JONNY: Out of all your female murder victims, want to know how many are found naked? All but two.

HOWARD: *(Beat.)* You know these stats pretty well for a paper you wrote a long time ago.

JONNY: The paper became a part of a lecture. Let's talk about race. Out of your sixteen characters of color that have a significant plot function across your work, want to know how many can dance? All of them!

HOWARD: I have read all of James Baldwin. You may have heard of him. He's a black, gay, American, canonical novelist. You know what he writes about a lot? How well black people dance! How well they fuck! So fuck you! You want to write about prejudice! Write about your mother! Write about her understanding of good and evil! But obscure little journals don't want to attack black women, they've got it out for straight white men, such an easy target for the academy, well I'm sick of it! You want to rebuild the world in your own fucking image then build it! Don't throw stones at my world, I did the best I could. *(Beat.)* Jesus, kid. You have been treated like a member of this family your whole life and you call me prejudiced?

JONNY: You never treated me like a member of your family.

HOWARD: You're kidding.

JONNY: I *never* felt welcome. Not when you were in the room. I cut my knee. Lucinda gave me a band-aid. "Thank you, Lula," I said, because that's all I'd heard anybody call her. You said, "Actually, Jonny, Lula is a family name."

HOWARD: I have no memory of that.

JONNY: Charlotte brought home a guy she was dating. I came for dinner, you turned to him and you said, "You make a good point, son." You have *never* called me son.

HOWARD: That must be because I'm a sexist, homophobic racist.

JONNY: You called him "son." A tall, white, football-playing stranger.

HOWARD: You're right –

JONNY: Well that's a first in this house.

HOWARD: I had a problem with you. And it had nothing to do with the color of your skin or what you like to do with your dick. My problem is that you are tricky. You never could look anyone in the eye and shake their hand and convey any sense that you were an honest and straightforward individual. That football player walked into the room and right away you could tell he had a sense of himself and I respected that.

JONNY: I was a messed up kid. I didn't know who I was.

HOWARD: That shit may fly with Charlotte, it doesn't work on me. You knew who you were. You were scared of it.

JONNY: Of course I was scared of it! I read your books! I read every book you ever wrote! And so did Charlotte! How did you describe the lesbian in *Snow on Peachtree Street?* Oh, yes. Cursed. No wonder Charlotte cut her wrists.

A moment for this to land. Then HOWARD lunges for JONNY.

HOWARD: *(To JONNY.)* You take that back! You take that back!

They fight. JONNY's stronger but HOWARD is angrier so they are evenly matched.

Eventually LUCINDA and CHARLOTTE enter. They carry garment bags containing wedding dresses.

LUCINDA: Wow!

CHARLOTTE: What the fuck?

JONNY has HOWARD pinned.

JONNY: If I let you go, will you stop?

HOWARD: Yes.

CHARLOTTE: What happened?

JONNY lets HOWARD go. HOWARD lunges again and gets JONNY in a headlock.

HOWARD: Take it back, take it back!

CHARLOTTE: *(At the same time.)* Stop it! Stop it! Stop it!

JONNY is starting to choke.

Dad!

Frightened and shocked, HOWARD releases JONNY, then leaves the room. Beat.

LUCINDA: Ice.

She exits. Pause.

JONNY: There's something I need to tell you. And it's going to upset you. But you will get over it.

CHARLOTTE: *(A little scared.)* I guess it upset my dad.

JONNY: *(A joke.)* Yeah, he's a little worked up.

CHARLOTTE: *(Not laughing.)* What did you do?

JONNY: Before I tell, I just want to remind you of something. Your Dad's books are a little racist, aren't they? And a little sexist. We've discussed this. Words for snow, remember?

CHARLOTTE: Did you say something nasty to him about his books?

JONNY: There's this class I taught. Teach. On popular fiction.

CHARLOTTE: About my dad?

JONNY: He's part of it. A big part of it.

CHARLOTTE: How long have you been doing that?

JONNY: A year. *(Beat.)* A couple of years.

Pause.

CHARLOTTE: Oh shit. *(Beat.)* Are we an illusion?

SCENE THREE

The Living Room. Day. Bright. CHARLOTTE is sitting, a laptop open. We hear JONNY's voice through the computer. Skype. Maybe we also see real JONNY. But crucial to keep the sense of distance and connections easily broken. CHARLOTTE is cold.

JONNY: You're over-reacting.

CHARLOTTE: Wrong.

JONNY: I've taken the article down. I've apologized.

CHARLOTTE: I don't want you there. It would upset me. It would upset my dad.

JONNY: I always looked up to your dad. Because he was a real writer and I wanted to be one too. Secretly.

CHARLOTTE: Of course. Secrets are your favorite thing.

JONNY: *(Ignoring this.)* And then I read his books. And I couldn't stop reading them. Even though they made me feel bad about myself. And I thought they might have made you feel that way too.

CHARLOTTE: In *real* life, not in books, in real life my father paid for camp and taught you fractions.

JONNY: If I had understood then that coming over to play came with so many strings attached I would have stayed home!

CHARLOTTE: Not strings. Loyalty.

JONNY: No, I'm being accused of biting the hand that feeds me. Guess what? I am not a dog.

CHARLOTTE: I let you share my family. You didn't even let me say goodbye to your mother.

JONNY: You're just like your dad, you know that? You're so fucking controlling. Well guess what? I'm a grown up independent man and if I want to stand up and say it like it is to a bunch of kids so that they don't have to grow up as scared as I did, and you should be supporting me, and happy for me, and proud of me, and if you can't be those things … *(He stops himself.)* But I'm also your best man and I love you.

CHARLOTTE: I don't know who you are. I want you to stop calling me. I want you to stop emailing. I want you to go away. *(Beat.)* OK?

HOWARD enters, in his dressing gown. He guesses she's talking to JONNY and freezes for a moment. HOWARD has aged a thousand years since the fight with JONNY.

JONNY: No that is not OK.

CHARLOTTE closes her laptop. No more JONNY.

CHARLOTTE: *(Brightly, to HOWARD.)* You want some coffee?

HOWARD: I'll get it. You want some more?

He heads to the kitchen – but before he goes:

Was that Jonny?

CHARLOTTE: That was the last of Jonny.

HOWARD: You guys have been friends a long time. I wouldn't want to be responsible –

CHARLOTTE: You're not.

(CHARLOTTE busies herself with something. HOWARD lingers.)

HOWARD: Charlotte, I just uh. You know, I – whatever I did, if I did something, I just want you to know how deeply, deeply, sorry I am. I just write. I never think about … I never considered …

CHARLOTTE: *(Not looking up.)* I barely read your books. Jonny's the one obsessed with them.

Pause.

HOWARD: You really don't want him at the wedding?

CHARLOTTE: No, because I've met someone for real now.

HOWARD: Who'll be your best man?

CHARLOTTE: I was going to ask you.

CHARLOTTE's cell phone starts to ring. She turns it off.

And Mom can give me away.

(HOWARD nods, uncertain.)

SCENE FOUR

A room at the Swallow's Lodge, with all the beige and tapestry that implies.

CHARLOTTE and LUCINDA are on the bed, clothed except for naked feet. Their toes are spread out by brightly colored foam separators, their toe nail is polish is drying. Pedicure accouterments are on the bed.

CHARLOTTE is tense.

LUCINDA: Night before *my* wedding I got high as a kite.

CHARLOTTE: Well I'm sober, so.

LUCINDA: From what Martha told me, she was the *real* alcoholic. Bottle of vodka, 10am.

CHARLOTTE: Let's change the subject.

LUCINDA: I joined the Peace Corps.

CHARLOTTE: You did? *(Beat.)* Isn't that for teenagers?

LUCINDA: Apparently my age is an advantage. A few weeks after you get back from your honeymoon I'll be leaving town for a while.

CHARLOTTE: Congratulations.

LUCINDA: I thank you.

Beat.

CHARLOTTE: I thought now that you're footloose and fancy free you might come up to D.C. and spend some time with us. We're talking about having a baby, you know. At some point.

LUCINDA: And at some point I'll be there. I promise you.

Pause.

The tux looks so sharp on you.

CHARLOTTE: Really?

LUCINDA: I get it now. It's very rock star.

CHARLOTTE: It's just a costume anyway. The whole thing is just costumes.

LUCINDA: Honey, do you not like the tux?

CHARLOTTE: I like it fine.

LUCINDA: Honey it's your wedding! You have to like the dress! Or the pant suit!

CHARLOTTE: I like it more than anything else I found.

LUCINDA: Oh honey, no! You have to feel beautiful on your wedding day.

CHARLOTTE: Martha's beautiful.

LUCINDA: I don't give a shit about Martha! I give a shit about you. Listen, I think the tux looks great but if you're not happy we will drive to a mall right now and I swear we will find something.

CHARLOTTE: I do like it. I do. I'm just nervous.

LUCINDA: There's nothing to be nervous about. You can always get divorced.

CHARLOTTE: I wish your sisters *weren't* coming. You should have checked with me before saying yes.

LUCINDA: I was excited they changed their mind.

CHARLOTTE: Everyone in the world is coming. Except Jonny.

LUCINDA decides not to comment on that.

CHARLOTTE: Nothing's how it was supposed to be. Nothing. You and Dad aren't together. I'm marrying a woman. The whole thing's just going to look weird.

LUCINDA: Honey, weird is good. I promise you. You think it didn't look weird when God created the world? There was all that nothingness and then ... what the fuck is all of that? Weird is life. Take a close look at a fish. Weird.

Beat.

CHARLOTTE: You said you didn't want to perform for me, remember?

LUCINDA: Yes.

CHARLOTTE: So, I know you and Dad are disappointed that I'm not marrying a guy.

LUCINDA: I can't imagine a guy in the world as special as Martha.

CHARLOTTE: Dad's disappointed. He's being really big about it, but he wanted me to marry that football player. Or that movie star.

LUCINDA: Dad was going to be disappointed in whoever you married. He is a Jew. There is never *not* a problem.

Pause.

CHARLOTTE: Carol *is* a mouse. I wish she wasn't coming to the wedding.

LUCINDA: You're going to have such a good time tomorrow you won't even know she's there.

CHARLOTTE: Are you seeing anyone?

LUCINDA: Unlike your dad, I feel no need for companionship. Between now and forever all I want are short, sharp bursts of life.

CHARLOTTE: What does that mean?

LUCINDA: I'm seeing several people.

CHARLOTTE: *(Taking this in.)* Do you meet them online?

LUCINDA: Hell no, I do it the old fashioned way. Bars and supermarkets. Making up for lost time. I'm fifty years old.

I'm not ready to put my orgasm in a drawer. I wasn't ready when I was thirty-five either.

Beat.

CHARLOTTE: Did you guys really not have sex for fifteen years?

LUCINDA: I don't want to tell tales out of school here –

CHARLOTTE: Good, that's best.

LUCINDA: But the very last time we did it, August 4th, seven summers ago, he stopped in the middle because he was trying to remember a telephone number. *(Beat.)* It's funny but it's not funny.

CHARLOTTE: *(Beat.)* I'm torn between wanting more details and wanting a more significant mother-daughter boundary.

LUCINDA: I know, right? It's so hard to know when to be mother and daughter and when to be friends. I'll follow your lead.

CHARLOTTE: Was Dad just not *capable*?

LUCINDA: Don't marry a writer, honey. All that time alone, with a computer. I'd check his browser history. Oh, he was capable.

Beat.

CHARLOTTE: I want us to be friends.

Beat.

LUCINDA: Walking through that house after you left for college, you know what I kept thinking about? My sister Stephanie's cat. And how it died. It died a month after she went to college. And it was odd because it was in perfect health, the prime of life. Nobody knew what the hell happened. But I knew. That cat died because no one in that house gave a damn about it after my sister had gone.

You were gone. Your father was writing. And I could not stop thinking about that dead cat.

CHARLOTTE: You sure it wasn't something it ate.

LUCINDA: It was an absence of love.

CHARLOTTE: But Dad does love you. He still loves you.

LUCINDA: But he's not *in* love with me. He's not in love with Carol either. He just likes someone waiting for him. In the other room.

CHARLOTTE: You stayed so long because of me, didn't you?

LUCINDA: I almost left one time. Well you know all about that.

CHARLOTTE: Do I? No I don't. What?

LUCINDA looks at her confused.

When did you almost leave?

LUCINDA: That night. That night you ...

CHARLOTTE: Oh.

LUCINDA: You knew that. That was why ... You heard us. Fighting about me leaving.

CHARLOTTE: I don't remember.

LUCINDA: The psychiatrist said you knew I was leaving and you freaked out. He blamed me.

CHARLOTTE: I didn't know that. We drove home in silence. We never talk about this.

LUCINDA: We're discussing it now.

CHARLOTTE: I don't want to. It's the night before my wedding.

LUCINDA: I apologize.

CHARLOTTE: I don't even know how we got onto this.

LUCINDA: We eliminated a boundary.

CHARLOTTE: Oh right.

LUCINDA: Let's put it right back up.

CHARLOTTE: You should not have blamed yourself. He should not have blamed you. I didn't say anything like that. I didn't say hardly anything at all. You must have told him you were fighting. He asked me if that was why. I said yes. It was just easier. I wanted to get out of there. Shit!

CHARLOTTE has messed up the drying nails on one of her feet.

LUCINDA: I'll take care of it.

She takes CHARLOTTE's foot in her lap and re-beautifies the nail.

I love that your nail polish is your something blue. *(No response.)* We got too serious didn't we, and we shouldn't have. That's my fault. *(Beat.)* When you were a little girl and you got sad do you remember what I'd do?

CHARLOTTE: *(Grim.)* Don't do it.

LUCINDA lunges at CHARLOTTE.

LUCINDA: Tickle tickle tickle!

She tickles CHARLOTTE and CHARLOTTE can't help laughing. The tickle-tussle becomes a very tight hug.

CHARLOTTE: Now you've messed up both our nails.

LUCINDA: Let's start again.

She takes CHARLOTTE's foot, and removes all the nail polish. She does not look up as:

CHARLOTTE: I told Whitney I was in love with Jasmine. But that was dumb because Whitney told Ashley and Kayla. And Jasmine. And they came and found me in the bathroom at recess. And they asked me about it. "I never said I was in *love* with Jasmine. I said I loved her." That's what I said, quick as a flash. And I saw them consider this little word "in" and whether or not it made a difference. And I was thinking about it too, was leaving out that one word going to save me? And then Kayla said, "If you didn't say it then why are you about to cry? There are tears in your eyes." I said, "No, there's not." But there were. And they were about to spill out. Then Kayla said, "Blink." And the three of them were just staring, waiting. So I blinked. And somehow the lid of my eye pushed back the tears. Nothing ran down my face. I thought God saved me. Now I have to change. That night I decided to become an Orthodox Jew and slept like a baby. The next morning I walked to the bathroom and cut my wrists. It had nothing to do with you and Dad fighting. It had to do with me realizing there was a major problem with the way I fell in love.

Pause. Really long.

LUCINDA: *(Firmly.)* Well there is no way you could have handled a divorce. Not with all that going on.

CHARLOTTE: No one knows that story except Martha.

LUCINDA: Not Jonny?

CHARLOTTE: Jonny was the only kid at school who never asked me why. That was one of the things I liked about him.

Knock at the door.

LUCINDA: *(Calling out.)* It's open!

HOWARD enters. He's carrying a big box.

HOWARD: Surprise! *(To LUCINDA.)* You could have stayed at the house.

CHARLOTTE: She thinks this is Bohemian.

LUCINDA: *(At the same time.)* This is Bohemian. You're intruding.

HOWARD: I know, but I did a thing and I didn't know if it would come off but it has. Maybe. *(To CHARLOTTE.)* I know you don't love the tux. And although I absolutely think it's great if you want to wear a tux I have been on a hunt this last month and the hunt has come to an end.

He hands her the box.

You don't have to like it, you don't have to wear it. But this was your mother's wedding dress. Which, in an attempt to send a message to me, not caring how it affected her only child, she sold on eBay to a woman in Oregon. Said woman, since purchasing the damn dress, now lives off the grid and it was quite a challenge to track down her earthship. However, I don't write detective fiction for nothing. I succeeded. I bought back the dress at twice the price, please note how this woman professes to live outside the capitalist system but in fact is an exemplar of said system. The dress arrived, by FedEx an hour ago. And if you want to wear it a lady will come by the house and do alterations in the morning. You're welcome.

LUCINDA: *(To HOWARD.)* I remember you. Didn't we fall in love?

HOWARD: *(To CHARLOTTE.)* You don't have to wear it honey. It's just another option. But it will look great. It looked great on Bob Dylan over there.

He means LUCINDA.

CHARLOTTE: You don't think two dresses will look weird?

HOWARD: No!

LUCINDA: *(At the same time.)* You need to get over that! Go try it on.

CHARLOTTE: I make no promises.

LUCINDA: Do what you want, we love the tux.

CHARLOTTE exits to the bathroom.

God bless you, I hate that fucking tux. Although of course, if she was transgendered, nothing but support. Jesus, having kids is exhausting.

HOWARD: *(Through the bathroom door, to CHARLOTTE.)* Listen, Jonny came by the house. *(Beat.)* He's in town. He's in town specifically in case you change your mind.

Pause.

LUCINDA: You wouldn't be this mad at him if you didn't love him, honey. Hate and love are totally connected.

HOWARD: *(To LUCINDA.)* Really? Tell it to the Nazis. *(To CHARLOTTE.)* You're not keeping Jonny away on my account I hope. Because I have forgiven him. He opened my eyes in a way. *(To LUCINDA.)* Did she tell you? I'm pitching a new series to my publishers. Lead character. Black lesbian. A former prostitute. My agent loves it. And so does HBO. *(HOWARD checks CHARLOTTE's out of earshot.)* Jonny changed the title of his book from *Letters I Never Wrote My Mother* to *Letters I Never Wrote*. There's four letters to me in there. He gave them to me.

LUCINDA: And?

HOWARD: They're very moving. You know he never knew his biological father and sometimes he'd pretend it was me. But it was complicated too because I was white and he didn't want a white father and also he was kind of attracted to me.

LUCINDA: He was *not*.

HOWARD: It's implied. There's a whole section about him wanting me to muss his hair and it's deliberately and interestingly quasi-sexual.

LUCINDA: Says you.

HOWARD: He had powerful emotions surrounding me. There's a whole section where he describes beating me, almost to

death. It's great. He really goes there. I had a son. I had a
son this whole time.

LUCINDA: Howard, he's not *actually* your son.

HOWARD: Of *course* he was a little off. He's a writer. Writers
are *off*. I am *off*.

LUCINDA: That's one word for it.

HOWARD: He wrote letters to Charlotte. Said he mailed them.
(Loud.) Did you get Jonny's letters honey?

LUCINDA: She wants to be focused on Martha. And that's
quite right.

HOWARD: A wedding is let bygones be bygones time. Even
your sisters have figured that out.

LUCINDA: Listen, it breaks my heart. Everything seemed right
with the world when I watched those two kids play under
the tree. I'd turn off the radio so I could hear them laugh.
They were beautiful. But they were kids.

HOWARD: Carol and I aren't really going around the world
you know. I mean, she wants to but …

LUCINDA: You'd rather be working.

HOWARD nods.

HOWARD: Maybe we'll take a short trip. I don't know.

CHARLOTTE: *(From the bathroom.)* Mom, can you come in and
button me up?

HOWARD: *(To CHARLOTTE, excited.)* How's it look?

LUCINDA: I'm going to see her in that dress and cry like a
baby.

HOWARD: Me too. *(Beat.)* See? I did something right.

LUCINDA gives him a hard kiss on the lips.

LUCINDA: We did a lot of things right.

LUCINDA enters the bathroom.

(From the bathroom.) Howard get in here! Get in here and see how beautiful she looks!

SCENE FIVE

Under the tree. Night. At the front of the house, the wedding. Somewhere else, colored lights. Somewhere else laughter. Somewhere else music. Here, mostly darkness. Quiet.

HOWARD leads CHARLOTTE by the hand. She's in her wedding dress, laughing.

CHARLOTTE: What? What's so important? I'm supposed to be mingling …

HOWARD: I have something for you.

CHARLOTTE: I didn't know you could be so happy! I didn't know!

She hugs her father.

HOWARD: Listen, listen. I want this to be a perfect day.

CHARLOTTE: It has been!

HOWARD: I don't want you to look back and feel like something was missing.

CHARLOTTE: Like what?

HOWARD: Jonny.

JONNY appears from the shadows. He's in a suit.

JONNY: Yes?

HOWARD: No, I wasn't cueing you, I was saying you were what was missing.

JONNY: *(Worried.)* Sorry.

CHARLOTTE: Why is he here?

HOWARD: No you listen to me. You hear me out. You love this young man – yes you do. You *do*. My dad's out there. And I'll tell you something, I hate my father. I *hate* him. But I love him. And I needed him to come tonight. There are going to be photos. This is forever. *I'm* the one Jonny wrote about. I have forgiven him. He has forgiven me for nearly choking him to death. In fact we're quite close now.

JONNY nods. The two men put their arms around each other's shoulders, demonstratively.

I would like to dance with the closest thing I have to a son at your wedding.

CHARLOTTE: Too bad.

CHARLOTTE starts to exit, JONNY runs after, grabs her hand.

JONNY: Would you just hear me out? You don't answer my calls, you don't write back to my emails.

CHARLOTTE: I don't read them. I have to get back. I've left Martha talking to a horrific aunt I never met.

HOWARD discreetly exits.

JONNY: Stephanie? You did meet her once. There was a very awkward tea years ago. You forced me to attend.

CHARLOTTE: It's great that you and my dad are best buds now, but I gotta go.

JONNY: I don't give a shit about your dad. I give a shit about you.

CHARLOTTE: Our whole thing, it was a joke, it was an act. I look back at us, I feel so sad. Two frightened little kids hiding away from other people and pretending to be soul mates because they thought they needed each other. Because they had to hide. *(Beat.)* I didn't *understand* I could have a wedding. I never knew I could have a life partner, one that I really wanted. One that I loved completely. One that wouldn't cower in the corner when I took my clothes off.

JONNY: Great. Now you know. You still need friends. We can't be friends until you forgive me.

CHARLOTTE: Look, I forgave you for letting me go through all that coming-out *shit* alone when we could have gone through it together.

JONNY: *(Off her tone.)* See I don't think you really did.

CHARLOTTE: Because, you're a fucking coward! I came out to my parents, you waited until your mother was dead.

JONNY: And do you have any idea how much I regret that? You know that you're loved unconditionally. I don't know that. I haven't had that yet. She never knew who I was!.

JONNY's voice breaks. It looks like she's about to see him cry for a second time.

CHARLOTTE: I don't trust you any more. You're a locked-up filing cabinet and you swear there's nothing important inside and then out of nowhere you'll pull out some incredibly important document and say, "Oh I'm sorry. This was in here all along, but it doesn't mean anything." But it does mean something. What you keep inside is who you fucking are and you never told me what was inside. You barely let me inside your house!

JONNY: Charlotte, I've been lying my entire life. To everyone! I'm trying to get better. You're walking away while I'm trying to get better? I do love you completely. If we were straight I'd kiss you now, to make you believe me. But we're not so I don't have that option. So I've only got words. And I don't know how to arrange the alphabet the right way to make you believe me.

CHARLOTTE: I have to get back to Martha.

JONNY: Pah!

JONNY has executed a dance move. I don't know if it's Liza doing Fosse or Travolta in Saturday Night Live but it is a bold gesture. CHARLOTTE stares. She loves him.

CHARLOTTE: What is that?

JONNY: That is dance.

And then, as fast as he can, JONNY undresses. CHARLOTTE continues to stare.

CHARLOTTE: And what is this?

JONNY: This is only fair.

CHARLOTTE: I have to go. Martha –

JONNY: Martha will be fine. She's amazing, remember? You couldn't find a better partner, blah blah blah. She's the best. She's Jewish. She's a doctor. She can dance. But we're *us*, remember?

He's down to his underwear.

CHARLOTTE: Don't.

JONNY: I understand that what I'm about to show you will repel you. But you showed me yours.

He takes off his underpants.

This is me. And this is me dancing.

He dances for her. She stares, softening.

Everyone assumes homosexuals can dance too. I really labor under a tremendous amount of stereotypes and expectations.

HOWARD's FATHER enters under the tree. At first he doesn't see them. They see him and freeze. He lights a cigarette, turns and sees CHARLOTTE and naked JONNY: The cigarette falls from his lips. Pause.

CHARLOTTE: Grandpa, I don't think you ever met my friend, Jonny. *(Clarifying the situation.)* Nothing's going on here. He's a homosexual.

HOWARD's FATHER beats a hasty retreat. CHARLOTTE and JONNY look at each other.

Maybe you should …

JONNY: Yeah.

JONNY puts on his underpants.

CHARLOTTE: You're here.

JONNY: Yeah …

They move towards each other. They hug. At the front of the house where the wedding guests we never see are, muffled by the distance, a song starts. A classic.*

The whole day I wanted to gatecrash, like this was a romantic comedy.

CHARLOTTE: *(A wail.)* I wanted to ask you if I should have worn the dress or the tux. And you missed the ceremony and we can never get that back.

JONNY: I was in my mom's yard. I wore a suit. I stood up. I was silent. *(Beat.)* I was present.

They dance.

CHARLOTTE: Martha can lead. I told her I hated dancing and normally she lets me alone but one time, early on, she just swooped in while I was in the middle of a conversation and she held me just so and somehow she danced me right across the room. And my feet knew what they were doing. And I couldn't stop laughing.

JONNY: Will's obsessed with rollercoasters.

*See Music Use Note on Copyright Page.

CHARLOTTE: You're still with Will …

JONNY: I went on one with him. Afterwards I threw up, but I did.

HOWARD and LUCINDA rush out.

HOWARD: What the hell's happening out here?

LUCINDA: Jonny, put your clothes back on!

CHARLOTTE and JONNY keep swaying.

HOWARD: That is so beautiful.

He moves to join them.

LUCINDA: Howard, leave them be. Jeez-Louise …

HOWARD is in the circle.

JONNY: *(To HOWARD.)* Oh. Hello.

HOWARD: Come join us, Lula. The night is young, the moon is full –

LUCINDA: The wedding is that way. And we are not being gracious hosts.

But as she's talking, HOWARD goes to get her. She resists but just a little.

HOWARD: And we will not pass this way again.

LUCINDA is in the circle.

CHARLOTTE: *(To LUCINDA.)* And hello to you. Welcome.

Beat. The family becomes a swaying circle. Until:

I've got to go. Martha will be pissed. Put on your clothes and come join.

CHARLOTTE exits. JONNY hurriedly dresses.

HOWARD: I shall go placate my father.

He exits.

LUCINDA: This time in three weeks I'll be in Uzbekistan. *(Off JONNY's look.)* I joined the Peace Corps. It wasn't my first choice, but whatever. I'll miss this air.

She looks at JONNY for a response but he's busy dressing.

Time, time, time, time, time. Jesus Christ. I feel so fucking free.

JONNY is close to dressed now. He approaches LUCINDA, ready to take her back to the wedding. He checks his shirt.

JONNY: I hope I didn't get grass stains on this.

LUCINDA: Hey.

JONNY: What?

LUCINDA: Love ya, kid.

JONNY stares at her. He smiles. Abrupt blackout.

End of play.

www.ingramcontent.com/pod-product-compliance
Ingram Content Group UK Ltd.
Pitfield, Milton Keynes, MK11 3LW, UK
UKHW031249020325
455689UK00008B/135